DESIGN STUDIO
2023 VOLUME 6

Design Studio Vol. 6 Collective Action! The Power of Collaboration and Co-design is printed on White Offset 300gsm and White Offset 120gsm paper, FSC®. Papers Carbon Balanced by the World Land Trust. Printed with eco-friendly high-quality vegetable-based inks by Pureprint Group, the world's first carbon neutral printer.

Published by RIBA Publishing,
66 Portland Place, London, W1B 1AD

ISBN 978 1 914124 90 7

British Library Cataloguing-in-Publication Data

A catalogue record for this book is available from the British Library.

Commissioning Editor: Alex White
Assistant Editor: Clare Holloway
Production: Marie Doinne
Designed and typeset by Linda Byrne
Printed and bound by Pureprint Group Ltd
Cover design: Linda Byrne

www.ribapublishing.com

FSC www.fsc.org
RECYCLED
Paper made from recycled material
FSC® C022913

ARTICLES

ACTIVISM PROFILES

PRACTICE CASE STUDIES

About the Editors

Rob Fiehn is a London-based freelance communications consultant, dedicated to professional and cultural activities within the architectural community. He works alongside architects, designers and institutions, with a career spanning books, exhibitions, concepts, thought leadership, profiling and events. Rob is currently the Chairman of the Board of the Museum of Architecture, a committee member of the London Society, a board director for the Blackhorse Workshop in Walthamstow and a trustee of the DKUK gallery in Peckham.

Kyle Buchanan is a director at Archio and a passionate and skilled architect, who was named RIBA South West Project Architect of the Year 2018. He is a RIBA Conservation Registrant with experience of working on listed buildings and in heritage contexts. His expertise in housing design has resulted in his appointment as a member of the RIBA Expert Advisory Group for Housing and as a Design Council Expert.

Mellis Haward is a director at Archio and has led many of Archio's housing and community projects. With her expertise in urban design, listed buildings and planning policy, she is a member of the Harrow, Hounslow and Tower Hamlets Design Panels, and the Hackney Regeneration Design Advisory Group, advising the councils on current applications and policy in the borough. She is also an AJ Architects Award Judge, Civic Trust Awards Assessor, a member of the Urban Design London Environmental Design Review Panel and a Design Council Specialist Expert.

Acknowledgements

The editors would like to thank the RIBA for supporting the concept of collaboration between architects, which resulted in the Guerrilla Tactics conference in 2021 and now this book. It shows that competing with one another doesn't compare to what can be achieved when we work together. With this in mind, it is important to recognise all the time, goodwill and energy that has been spent by the contributors to this publication, as they have created entirely new essays to help promote this positive aspect of the profession.

Collective Action!

The Power of Collaboration and Co-design

Editor's Introduction

Rob Fiehn

Collaboration in architecture is not a new thing. Buildings would not and could not be built without teams of people working together towards a common goal. Architects often have a privileged role in the process because they are brought in by a client to help them decide what form the project should take, how it is presented to the local community, the various stages of evolution it needs to go through to get planning, and then (hopefully) how it should be built. But many other parties and professionals – involved in areas such as structural engineering, acoustics, drainage, lighting and so on – have to combine to produce structures that adhere to proper guidance and regulation. However, the architect's position in this whole system is shifting and has been for some time. Various responsibilities have been eroded over the last few decades, sometimes reducing the role of the architect to a project manager or design facilitator. This loss of autonomy is being questioned by a generation of practitioners, and they're finding strength in numbers. Collaboration, it turns out, is a great way to communicate ideas, engage with the general public and produce projects by groups that far exceed the sum of their parts. This collegiate approach to design shrugs off the 20th-century notion of the lone genius in favour of a more practical and effective form of architecture that provides greater diversity and a plurality of voices – something that has long been missing from the profession.

Where this book started

In 2021, Mellis Haward, Kyle Buchanan and I were given the opportunity to programme the RIBA Guerrilla Tactics conference, which was named 'Stop, Collaborate and Listen'. The purpose of this event was to show small practices that they could achieve so much more if they pooled resources and experiences. It proposed that information about materials, new technologies, zero-carbon construction and best business practice should be made easily available from peers, without the need to worry about competitive behaviour. It presented a bright future for architects if practices could unite to win work or to level up their skills. Speakers came from a wide range of different backgrounds across the length and breadth of the UK, and included both the private and public sectors. Examples of collaborative working were presented by large studios and micro-practices, activists and academics. It tapped into the recent growth of collectives that have formed to help architects deal with issues that are usually outside their control or fall into the knowledge gap. The conference was heralded as a

Left: The 2021 Guerrilla Tactics conference artwork.

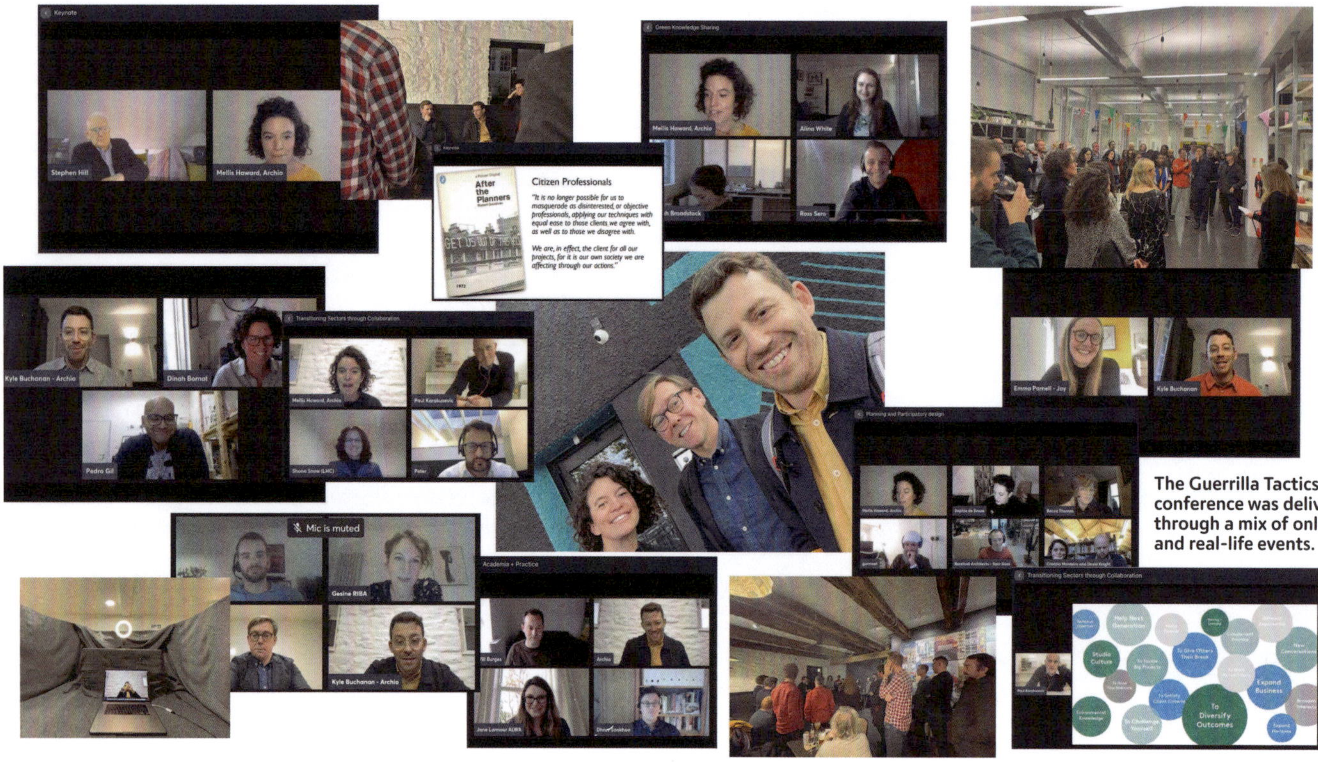

The Guerrilla Tactics conference was delivered through a mix of online and real-life events.

success and, despite the fact that it was delivered mostly virtually, it created a sense of unity that has persisted. It inspired the creative directors and RIBA Publishing to produce this book, drawing on many of the same themes and issues that were covered in the conference but providing the opportunity to go into more detail about how such teams and projects are developed.

What's in it?

The editors were inspired by the many different forms of collaboration that are taking place around the world. The intention of this book is to shine a light on a number of key areas where collaboration is allowing architects to rethink old methods and draw on collective energy. Dhruv Adam Sookhoo uses his chapter 'Strategies for collaborative research in architectural practice' to explore how academic methods of research can produce tangible results within a practice, demonstrating the knock-on effects for the business as findings are shared publicly through exhibitions, events and articles. Archio – making up two-thirds of the editors of this book – have spent years honing their skills working with communities to produce designs and methods of engagement that ensure projects are integrated into their surroundings and welcomed by the local population, which is unpacked in 'Co-design tools'. In 'Getting to grips with embodied carbon', Feilden Clegg Bradley Studios outline how their carbon calculator works and the reasons why they felt they had to share it with the world, as we unite to tackle the growing threat of the global climate emergency. Their freely available tool has been downloaded over 3,500 times. WIP is a New York-based collective of female practitioners who realised they could produce work together to make the city a more accessible and inclusive place. 'Community and collaborative' shows that by gathering their different skills and learning from similar groups from the past (such as the Matrix Feminist Design Co-operative) they can create projects like Restorative Ground, a new kind of urban landscape that welcomes neurodiversity. Collective Work's chapter 'In-sourcing' describes how their practice was formed with a sense of the power of shared efforts. They started their studio with a network of architects and consultants that they could draw on for a huge range of potential projects. This approach has then formed the basis for the way that they collaborate with clients and communities, developing into a thread of working methods that runs through everything they do. New Practice are based in Glasgow but their reach extends across the whole of the UK. The team is modest in size but together members are able to punch above their weight thanks to a collaborative approach, which they explain in 'Building a dream team' through gradations of scale: 1:1 is the intimate start of things, working with an individual, and they reach all the way up to 1:100,000, reflecting city making at a strategic level. David Ogunmuyiwa uses his chapter on 'Collaborative delivery' to uncover how the process of small and large practices working together actually delivers results. He talks with his collaborative partner, Paul Karakusevic, about the benefits of gathering different voices around the table to enrich a project and see it through different perspectives.

Profiles and case studies

This book also includes a series of profiles and case studies of practices and collectives that reveal the rich variety of collaboration that is currently being embraced by the profession both in the UK and abroad. They stand as a testament to the old adage of an organisation being 'more than the sum of its parts' but also show what individuals can do when they seek help. For instance, the Architects Climate Action Network (ACAN) is growing into an international group with a shared goal and a host of activities, while Paradigm Network is a more localised professional network that supports diversity in the built environment, and then there's the inspirational Amy Francis-Smith, who campaigns for better provision for people across the spectrum of disability, often partnering with larger organisations and groups.

Lacol is a cooperative of architects from Barcelona in Spain. They have written about their La Borda project, which represents a community-based self-development model to provide shared living, showing what happens when future residents are allowed to be a part of the design process. Retrouvius is a reclamation and design studio that partners with architects to create beautiful projects, such as the Tennis Court House, that celebrate reuse through materials, fixtures and fittings. The POoR Collective (Power Out of Restriction) created the Bringing Home to the Unknown installation in Regent's Park by working with Year 10 students from a nearby school, using co-design processes. The book is closed by Stephen Hill in the 'Final word' essay. Stephen is a co-production expert, and he argues for a future where architects are even more collaborative, abandoning the concept of the 'perfect moment' of a complete project, and instead embracing the idea that they are really providing a foundation for communities to continue the design process through occupying the space.

This wouldn't truly be a book on collaboration without crowdsourcing some thoughts from others. We reached out to the Collaborative Summit, a new group trying to explore the benefits of collaboration for business and social purposes. This is what some of them had to say:

Jonathan Hagos, FREEHAUS

Design can be an isolating experience. With each project comes a new agenda, a new client, and to remain steady and true we can all too easily construct a narrative and a safe structure of consultants and working processes which, like an echo chamber, appears to make objective our subjectivity and validates our every move.

Collaborating has helped us avoid the well-trodden path, to be brave and to be exposed; exposed to a different rhetoric, to a different methodology and to a new set of tools.

Above all, working collaboratively (with other architects in particular) has directed us into new arenas – ones with different challenges but with meaningful support to help us navigate them.

At a more human scale, each collaboration brings with it a platform for new voices and ideas. These differing voices can align and, yes, they can often clash, but then every once in a while, they can spark something new and create the unexpected. Paramount to this is a respect for the journey that each of us has been on and our unique experiences which give rise to our creative voice: 'all has been given to us as raw material, like clay, so that we may shape our art'.

Lanre Gbolade and Tara Gbolade, Gbolade Design Studio

We see collaboration as a key ingredient of our culture and therefore an inherent part of how our team works as a practice with other built environment disciplines. With the outputs of architecture being so wide-ranging and socio-economically impacting as well as environmentally, it is important to keep evolving and developing our practice through knowledge-sharing with other collaborative-minded practices.

We appreciate that other practices will have areas of strengths and expertise that might complement our regenerative design approach. In this, we find there is potential for a combining of efforts that enables design team members/practices to collaborate to widen our collective approaches to design, increase the innovation potential, punch above our weight and offer added value to our clients.

Critically, in agreeing any collaborative working relationships with other practices, we seek to clarify close alignment of practice and design values prior to starting projects and focus on ultimately achieving an additive rather than extractive process. As an example, we stipulate what our strengths are so our role on a project is aligned to these as much as possible.

Tim O'Callaghan, nimtim

As a small practice we recognised opportunities and the potential for growth were going to be limited without sharing and learning from other practices. As a result, we've nurtured specific collaboration projects but also collaborative networks where we share knowledge, recommendations and resources.

Each of these networks has a different character and focus. One grew around a specific area and type of work in London; another has a range of practice types and sizes and shares useful contacts and lessons of running a practice. We've recently brought together a group of practices with a specific focus on learning from collaborating with larger practices.

While we are often in direct competition with some of the other practices involved, there's a recognition that we have much more to gain by sharing resources and learnings than we have by keeping them to ourselves.

The recent trend for collaborative projects has not only improved individual practices but also the entire profession, as better ways of designing, working, thinking are shared and tested more widely.

Eddie Blake and Cliff Rogers (a Studio Weave collaboration)

Buildings are deeply emotive structures which form our psyche;[1] *they have that emotive power because they also come from our minds. They rarely, however, come from a single mind.*[2] *Architecture is a collaborative discipline.*[3] *It's all but impossible to unpick where architectural ideas come from – it's not as if any collaboration is properly footnoted.*[4] *Architects collaborate with other disciplines, with other architects – some architects even say they collaborate with the public. The sheer quantity of collective thought involved in architecture is remarkable, and, as you know, quantity has a quality all of its own.*[5] *Sometimes collaborations are the closest thing in the professional world to a romantic relationship.*[6] *As such, sometimes collaborations are a sham, and sometimes they're awful. Sometimes we even collaborate with the past, stealing old ideas – it can't help it, architecture's deepest compulsion is to repeat.*[7] *Collaborations teach us. Ultimately each collaboration leaves you with something – one taught me patience, one taught me pain.*

Let's work together

The editors of this book believe strongly that closer and more integrated forms of collaboration hold the keys to the future of the architectural profession. We're all better off when we share the load and find common ground. We hope this book showcases that across a multitude of different examples, in the UK and elsewhere. It's clear that if architects are to have any hope of effecting change in an extremely challenging world, then it will be together.

1 David Adjaye, quoted in Tom Dyckoff, '*Behind the facade*', Guardian, 8 February 2003, https://www.theguardian.com/artanddesign/2003/feb/08/architecture.artsfeatures (accessed 14 September 2022).

2 Eddie Blake, WhatsApp message, 13 May 2022.

3 Charles Holden, quoted in Alan Powers, '*Holden, Charles (Henry)*', Grove Art Online, Oxford University Press, 2007.

4 Professor Kester Rattenbury, personal email, 18 May 2022.

5 Attributed variously to Mao, Lenin or Trotsky.

6 JJ Cliff Rogers, *misheard* on Zoom.

7 Sam Jacob, *Make it Real: Architecture as Enactment*, Strelka Press, 2015.

Strategies for Collaborative Research in Architectural Practice:

Communicating Metropolitan Workshop's A New Kind of Suburbia

Dhruv Adam Sookhoo

Metropolitan Workshop testing alternative suburban configurations using a resin model of the Homestead for the ENGIE design manual, 2019.

Despite evidence that architects are increasingly conducting research in practice, few have published detailed accounts of their experience of designing and implementing research projects within commercial architectural practices. This represents a distinct barrier to establishing a shared culture of research within a profession that relies on learning through practice. This chapter considers *A New Kind of Suburbia*, a practice-based research project conducted by Metropolitan Workshop, before discussing strategies to enhance collaboration through research dissemination and shared research agendas. This is intended to complement guidance offered by others concerning research design, implementation and dissemination for shared learning in practice settings.[1] The case study and subsequent guidance considers the need to reconcile research with the commercial priorities of architectural practice. These insights are useful for architects undertaking practice-based research and, potentially, for academics wishing to collaborate with architects to define and implement their research agenda within commercial practice.[2]

Undertaking research in architectural practice

Research in architectural practice is increasingly promoted internationally to advance the professional knowledge base, enhance business practice and evidence the value of the architecture profession.[3] In the UK, recent calls to expand research culture within the architecture profession resonate with initiatives by the RIBA dating back to the 1960s, which sought to articulate practitioner knowledge and bolster the architecture profession's position by influencing policymakers, attracting clients and aligning it with other disciplines in an increasingly competitive market.[4] Contemporary architects undertake practice-based research to stimulate innovation and develop their practice expertise, introduce novel thinking and attract new talent to their studios, advance their passion projects, and potentially generate commissioned research.[5] More radically, others participate in practice-based research to redefine the boundaries of the architecture profession, critique relationships between academic and practice knowledge production, and examine the potential of speculative research processes liberated from the constraints of the academic institutions.[6] An expanding collection of case studies demonstrates the capacity of practitioner research to generate valuable findings, recommendations and applications for architectural practice, the profession and the wider built environment.[7] Moreover, cases testify to the diversity of research across all scales of practice, with and without specialist research staff, or collaboration with academic institutions.

Architectural practice demands a great deal of practice-based research, and tends to blur boundaries between the research process and its prospective contributions to wider commercial objectives. This embeddedness is understandable given that practice research is part of a single creative endeavour, perhaps undertaken by the same architect or project team also responsible for everyday commercial practice. However, clarity about what constitutes research is necessary for

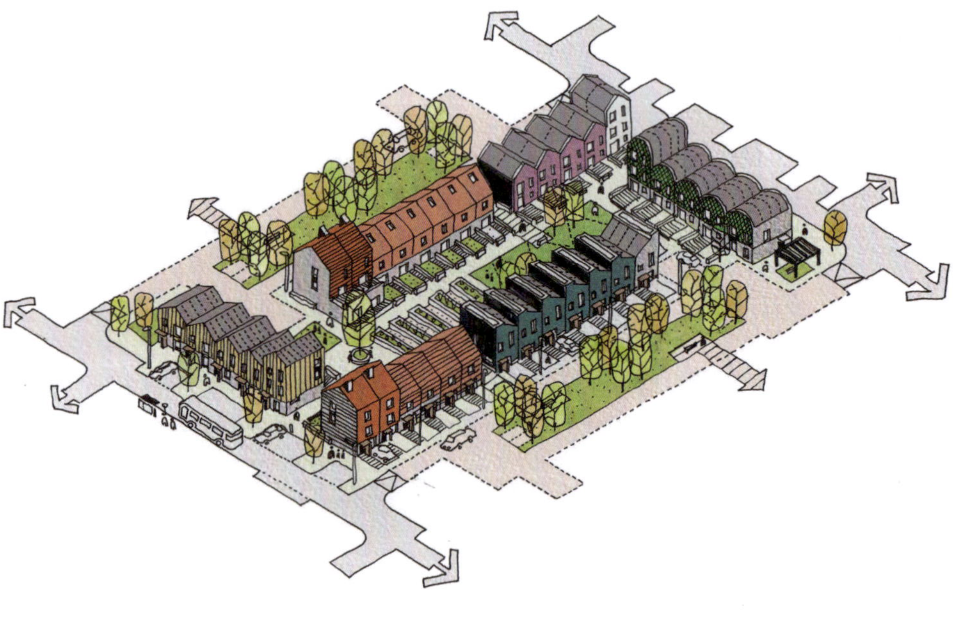

Metropolitan Workshop, the Homestead reinterpreted for modular construction for the ENGIE design manual, 2019. The Homestead concept was initially developed in collaboration with the late Sir Richard MacCormac in response to an RIBA ideas competition sponsored by the Wates Group in 2013. The successful entry proposed a new housing typology offering flexible homes and sociable neighbourhoods intended to meet the long-term aspirations of those privately renting in suburbia.

Metropolitan Workshop, the Homestead applied to Campbell Park North, Milton Keynes, for Urban Splash, 2017. Jesmonite resin model developed to communicate the potential for the Homestead to create a new type of suburban development capable of responding to changing markets and social conditions by enabling flexibility of density and tenure mix, and optimising private and public space to enhance the public realm.

research quality, developing collaborations that enhance research dissemination and application, and reconciling research processes with practice management to deliver organisational objectives (e.g., distinguishing speculative research from fee-earning practice).

Research is a systematic process of inquiry that generates new knowledge, or creatively analyses and synthesises existing knowledge, to produce original understanding or applications. To constitute research, an inquiry must collect and analyse relevant data using appropriate research methods, and document results (i.e., collecting relevant information without analysing it to generate communicable knowledge is not research). For example, gathering and exhibiting engaging data without undertaking analysis during its preparation and communicating this analysis in its presentation is unlikely to constitute research. Dissemination of research processes and outcomes is also critical if research is to shape professional practice knowledge and scholarly discourse.

Investment in practice-based research and effective dissemination are components of complex strategies adopted by architects to achieve distinction within competitive markets for architectural services and gain credibility to forge new collaborations within practice and academia. Practice-based research may not often translate directly into economic benefits (e.g., patents for new technological innovations), but it does offer a means of articulating enhanced and transformational technical, social, cultural and commercial expertise with the potential for economic reward (e.g., demonstrating added value during public procurement processes).[8] Findings and recommendations generated during practice-based research, when combined with architects' capacity to explain their practical application, represent an opportunity to create communication strategies of depth and relevance to a range of audiences. As one experienced practitioner explains, 'research under the auspices of … design practice can take many guises in terms of process and output', but it 'must translate into marketing and communications collateral'.[9]

Architects conducting research within their studios are well placed to examine and resolve intricate, ambiguous practice problems, because their pre-existing professional knowledge, familiarity with their workplace, and capacity to engage peers within practice communities as participants or collaborators offers an informed perspective from research design, through data analysis, to dissemination. This embeddedness offers architects undertaking practice-based research opportunities to access practice data and harness professional networks to gain feedback on research findings and recommendations, unavailable to most university-based academics. Potential drawbacks of undertaking practice-based research include difficulty adapting academic research methods to practice settings in order to demonstrate research quality, limited available academic literature on selected practice issues, undue influence of dominant professional or institutional approaches and discourses that may constrain innovation, and the absence of standardised procedures to support ethical research (e.g., managing confidentiality).

Practice research is exhilarating when it leads to personal development that enhances design practice, but it is time-consuming and labour-intensive, and may potentially distract practitioners from more routine, direct routes to professional recognition within architectural practice. Research processes can lead architects to uncover evidence and make recommendations that are difficult to reconcile with their personal values and professional identity, or produce conclusions that peers find difficult to accept (e.g., where research clarifies complicity with suboptimum practice or destabilises claims made by the profession).

Critical reflection can help architects account for potential biases and evaluate the effects of power relations on research design, data collection and analysis, and also findings and recommendations to enhance research quality and manage proximity innate in practice-based research.[10] But reflection is of limited practical benefit to early and mid-career researchers confronted by powerful practitioners resistant to the research process, or willing to influence it detrimentally. This can be mitigated if the potential for conflict is recognised, and researchers engage proactively with senior managers who act as organisational gatekeepers during early research design (e.g., when preparing research proposals). Success by early and mid-career practitioner-researchers hinges on the degrees of practical support afforded by senior managers such as access to knowledgeable colleagues and practice data, assistance to develop a research proposal and achieve organisational conformity with ethical requirements, and necessary paid time for analysis and writing.

Upfront, open negotiation between researchers, senior managers and external collaborators about the basis of their collaboration is necessary to avoid exploitation, promote trust and add value to research processes and outcomes.[11] This is particularly relevant where an employee has won their own research funds or is completing a research project as part of formal training endorsed by the practice. Collaboration during practice-based research should encourage architects without formal research training to participate and learn through the research process, enable the adaptation and modification of established research practices to achieve research quality within architectural practice, and generate communicable findings and recommendations useful to architects and practice collaborators. Put simply, collaboration within and without the profession during practice-based research should enhance research design and implementation, support the dissemination and application of research recommendations through relevant practice communities, and enable practice development through shared learning inside and outside the studio.

A New Kind of Suburbia: a case study of collaboration in practice-based research

Metropolitan Workshop was founded to examine 'the power of collaboration and creative exchange in the design process'.[12] This aspiration defined a shared vision for research among senior managements, which conceived research as a vehicle to promote dialogue with external designers, developers and policymakers, and a means to enhance design practice to address emerging issues. In 2019, Metropolitan Workshop committed to a research programme to enhance collaboration within and between studios in London and Dublin, and to enable the practice's commercial interests by supporting a developing communications strategy for external audiences and contributing to staff development.

Metropolitan Workshop's first extended research project, *A New Kind of Suburbia,* was completed in 2021. It sought to improve understanding of the challenges faced by existing and new suburban communities, and to enable design practice to harness social and technological innovations to enhance residents' quality of life. The project responded to the practice's expanding portfolio of suburban housing projects, and an existing interest in suburban innovation best demonstrated through the evolution and application of the Homestead as a typological device to multiple proposed built projects.[13]

The project began with the production of a working paper by the London studio, which framed project aims in relation to academic literature, emerging policy and market research, and assembled suburban precedents by the practice and leading architecture

Right: Metropolitan Workshop, A New Kind of Suburbia exhibition, London, 2019. The practice's London exhibition was designed by and mounted within its studio, and contributed to the Clerkenwell Design Week and London Festival of Architecture. Its partner exhibition in Dublin contributed to the Irish Architecture Foundation's Open House, October 2019.

Below: Metropolitan Workshop, Suburbia Making Architects, part of A New Kind of Suburbia exhibition, 14–16 Cowcross Street, London, 2019. Members of the studio were invited to prepare auto-ethnographic accounts of their formative experiences of suburban places, which were used to examine on how their aspirations for suburban places inform their design practice.

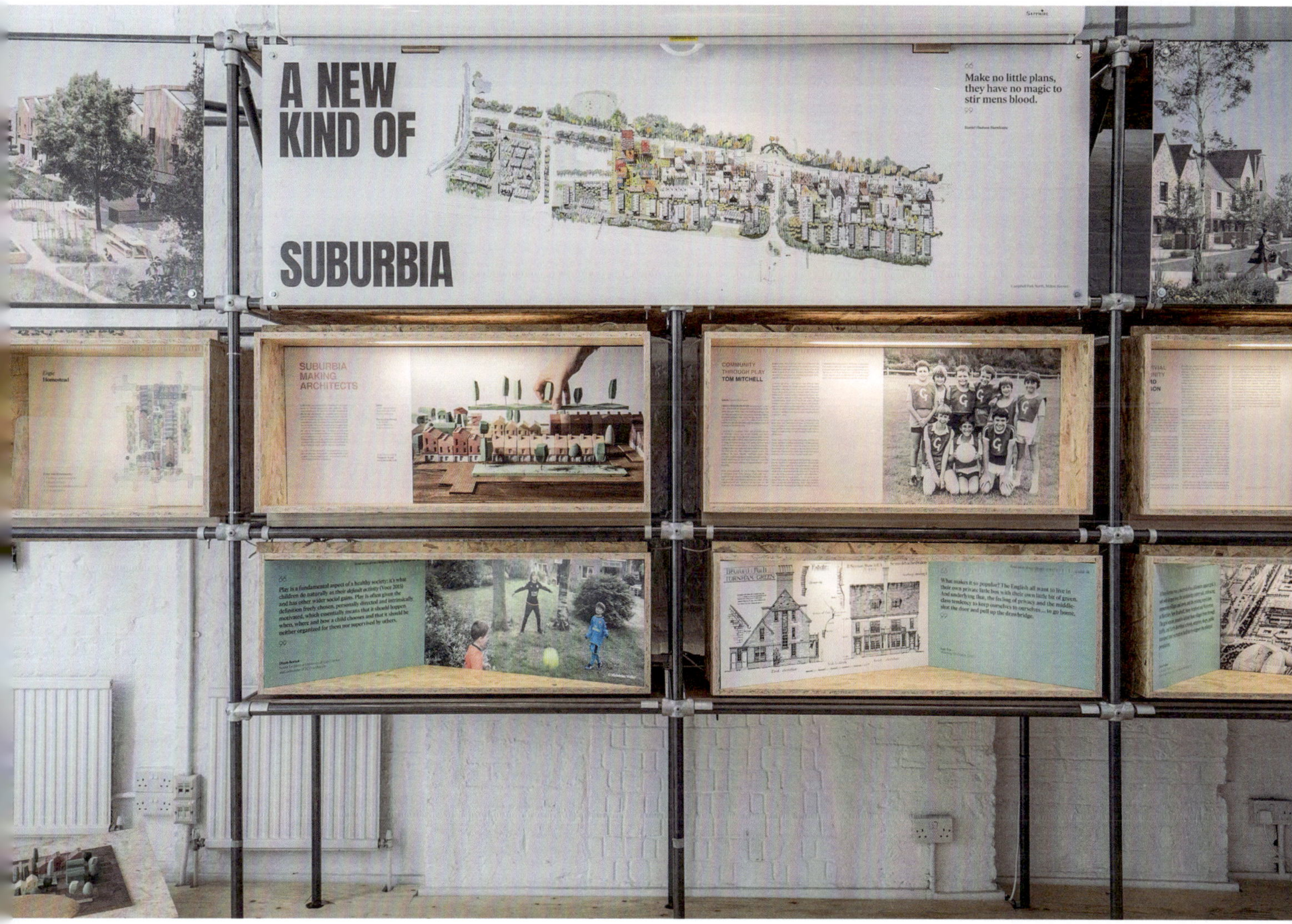

studios.[14] The working paper was the product of multiple qualitative methods of data generation and analysis, including interviews with industry experts, case studies examining current and future directions in suburban design and construction created inside and outside the practice, auto-ethnographic accounts by studio members of formative suburban experiences, and recollection of relevant writing.[15] This work was subsequently reinterpreted within the Dublin studio to better reflect the societal challenges and opportunities of suburban design and development in the Republic of Ireland.[16] Content developed within the working papers formed the basis of exhibitions held in Metropolitan Workshop's London and Dublin studios to coincide with national architecture events.[17] The practice invited exhibition talks by developers, academics, local authorities and design quality advocates to encourage critical thinking in relation to the production of current and future suburban places.[18]

Several participatory methods were used to disseminate initial insights and findings among peers, to refine analysis and recommendations by considering alternative industry perspective outside the practice, and to facilitate shared learning inside the practice. Most significantly, working papers, peer feedback on exhibitions and provocation in the form of exhibition talks provided a rich resource for a wide-ranging roundtable where invited practitioners and academics shared expertise in the production and use of suburban places. The roundtable generated new perspectives on Metropolitan Workshop's design practice, and identified productive intellectual trajectories for future practice-research and practice development.[19] Research and practice agendas emerging from critical discussion created a need to:

- challenge assumptions about suburban morphologies,
- examine suburban homes as sites of domestic consumption and production,
- mediate social inequality within suburban neighbourhoods by addressing inadequate infrastructure,
- enhance choice of suburban accommodation, and
- sustain shared semi-public spaces through community-led approaches.

These broad themes were reinterpreted and integrated into recommendations to form strategic questions to be considered when designing new suburban places or intervening in existing suburban neighbourhoods relating to: suburban intensification, sustainable transport, inclusive neighbourhoods, responsive typologies, choice of accommodation and the role of the housebuilder.[20] The research team recognised that the strategic nature of recommendations required additional interpretation to be beneficial for the everyday practice of the studio. So the project concluded with a practice-wide workshop, including contributions by external experts that explained the applicability of findings and recommendations from a range of practitioner perspectives.[21]

Metropolitan Workshop, A New Kind of Suburbia, 2019. The practice prepared an accessible, richly illustrated working paper to frame its thinking, refine analysis and drive collaboration in relation to suburban design and development, and act as a resource for participatory methods during the later phases of the research project.

Metropolitan Workshop distributed working papers in hardcopy at its exhibitions and through its website on an open-access basis, enabling promotion via social media.[22] Later, companion publications reporting research processes and resulting recommendations were circulated to practice collaborators. While managing intellectual property is an everyday consideration for commercial practice, research dissemination was essential to fulfil Metropolitan Workshop's intention of refining suburban design practices with peers. This commitment to collaboration extended to sharing ongoing evaluation of approaches to practice-based research used during *A New Kind of Suburbia*.[23]

Developing a shared culture of research in practice

A New Kind of Suburbia was an ambitious practice-based research project shaped by the commercial and social interests of the practice and its collaborators. It contributed to the strategic goals of an emerging research programme that sought to promote dialogue

Metropolitan Workshop, A New Kind of Suburbia exhibition, London, 2019. The exhibition was launched with a series of provocations by those responsible for producing suburban places. Taken together, the practice's working papers, exhibitions and invited provocations offered a rich resource for a stimulating and wide-ranging roundtable, with invited practitioners and academics with an interest in suburban housing.

with external collaborators to enhance the practice's response to emerging practice issues and develop approaches to practice research at Metropolitan Workshop that promote collaboration. The shared experience of delivering the research project created a collective understanding of the effort required to deliver an extended practice-based research project, and provided a shared model to evaluate and refine collaboration in subsequent projects. Reflection on the implementation of *A New Kind of Suburbia* generated valuable lessons for enhancing collaboration during practice-based research, including approaches to planning research strategies that deliver a shared vision for practice-based research, harness expertise within and outside the practice to enrich data analysis and generate recommendations applicable for future practice, and balance external dissemination with opportunities for practice development through shared learning.

Metropolitan Workshop's research programme developed organically, and continues to do so. *A New Kind of Suburbia* was a complex project, which enabled the evaluation of diverse approaches to research and dissemination for relative cost, effort and forms of expertise required, and the value of the outcomes for practice. This shared experience offered a realistic basis for planning future research projects within practice resource budgets, and compensates for the limited availability of cost information for delivering social research within practice settings.[24]

Planning research dissemination to recognise collaboration within studios

The impact of practice-based research is difficult to assess, as value materialises gradually from the application, evaluation and adaptation of new approaches through architectural practice and its networks. However, a straightforward means of determining whether research is valued in the short term is to test its reception with practice and academic audiences through publication.[25]

Practice knowledge uncovered during *A New Kind of Suburbia* was disseminated by Metropolitan Workshop through journal articles and invited chapters, contributions to professional training and university teaching, abridged articles for professional journals, and invited podcasts.[26] This list of research outputs is ordered to indicate reducing research impact, as judged from an academic perspective on

External contributors assemble for A New Kind of Suburbia roundtable, 2019.

the benefits of peer review.[27] However, the practice felt it essential to invest in forms of dissemination that were immediate and accessible to fellow and future professionals without economic barriers. Positively, open-access publication also enabled scholars to re-analyse and share Metropolitan Workshop's approaches to suburban intensification and community participation for healthier homes.[28]

While practice-based research may be commissioned in anticipation that findings and applications will enhance practice communication strategies, it is helpful for research quality and effective practice management to distinguish between data collection, analysis and reporting within the research team, and to avoid prioritising premature publicity. It is essential that sufficient, regular time is allocated for written analysis and dissemination within research teams at project milestones, to ensure research processes are adapted in an informed way and to aid shared learning. Sharing intermediate analysis and findings externally may be valuable if wider participation enables data collection, refines analysis and tests recommendations through peer feedback. However, any advantageous publicity generated should be considered secondary to benefits to the research process. This creates a tension between ensuring sufficient data collection and analysis has been undertaken to justify claims to new knowledge, and immediate commercial pressure to generate valuable media content. Arguably, this reflects a broader tension between practice-based design cultures that value immediacy of visual display, and academic approaches that demonstrate research quality through systematic, written analysis.[29]

Conflict between research and publicity objectives may be managed by developing a communication strategy that respects sequencing within research design, anticipates well-timed interim outputs, and creates platforms for dissemination that recognise the different requirements of practitioner and academic audiences. Communication strategies should also recognise that to be named as a co-author for a research output, it is necessary to make a significant contribution to research reported, and be accountable for its contents (i.e., sharing responsibility for resolving questions about the accuracy and integrity of published work).[30] Mere seniority within the research team or architectural practice is no guarantee of an authorship credit. Neither is the design and production of the output unless it explicitly constitutes a research method (e.g., exhibition design as a participatory practice). Discussing the criteria for authorship at project inception is useful for avoiding potential conflict given that architectural practices are structured by explicit and tacit hierarchies, and identifying authors may appear inconsistent with research processes promising collaboration. This is particularly relevant when collaborating with external academics. During *A New Kind of Suburbia*, the practice recognised the authorship of all contributing authors to edited publications, acknowledged external research participants, and identified studio members responsible for supporting the project through communications and graphic design. This research practice is intended to reflect the collaborative character of practice-based research, while identifying those responsible for creative research design and implementation.

Managing research programmes to enhance collaboration through practice management

Practice-based research occurs within studios governed by practice management processes necessary to ensure that creative architectural practice is professionally responsible and commercially viable. It is necessary to reconcile research projects with organisational strategies, to create opportunities for practice members to participate in research and dissemination. Metropolitan Workshop's continued expansion and creation of its permanent Dublin studio required research to plan more carefully to achieve collaboration for staff development and ensure projects contributed to other strategic and operational practice management objectives.

Systematically integrating research into the work of an architectural practice can begin by agreeing a shared mission statement for research with colleagues that explains the rationale for commencing a research programme, and how practice-based research will contribute to the broad vision for the practice.[31] Mission statements can be developed into a *strategic plan for research*, which outlines long-term and short-term objectives for the research programme; justifies the appropriateness of intended research projects against programme objectives; and identifies practice research leads, equitable approaches for enabling studio members to participate in research and criteria for external collaboration.

Adopting a transparent, structured approach to planning research can enable practices to align expected research outcomes to their commercial priorities (e.g., demonstrating expertise to enter new markets), relate research costs and sources of funding to practice finances (e.g., deciding to fund project-based research through fees or to seek external funding by bidding with an academic partner), avoid tensions between resourcing design projects and finding time for research (e.g., formalising approaches within human resources policies to release studio members to conduct research and dissemination), and anticipate the management of research ethics within a practice setting. Developing a robust organisational approach is also likely to be advantageous when preparing research proposals and assessing their feasibility and value to the practice.[32]

Practice managers will be reassured by planned research programmes, and corresponding project proposals, that demonstrate that interrelated business needs have been addressed, resources are appropriately allocated, and staff understand their responsibilities when conducting research. More innovative leaders will see the potential of developing research programmes collaboratively with practice representatives. Such inclusivity offers opportunities to identify shared interests, existing expertise and membership of networks; to agree commercial and social priorities for knowledge generation; and, importantly, to collectively commit to the work required to realise a 'research culture of architects'.[33] Collectively generating a research agenda and agreeing practical steps to achieve it enables studios to monitor progress together, evaluate the benefits and limitations of applying different research methods within their practice or research interest, and use shared judgement when deciding to deviate from their research plan to capture unexpected opportunities. Metropolitan Workshop diverted resources to respond to an opportunity to collaborate with leading academics to examine homeowner aspirations, because it built research capacity within the practice and generated publications related to a growing expertise in modern methods of construction for housing.[34]

Establishing a shared commitment to research culture is essential for practices to ensure that their research projects and the knowledge they generate enrich their wider creative endeavour. For smaller and emerging practices, developing a detailed, written strategic research plan may only become necessary as research practice gains momentum, and a plan is required to coordinate research within practice management, and communicate the value of research processes and outcomes to new studio members and those outside the practice's research culture.

A pragmatic first step for any size of practice embarking on a research project or programme is to use the structure of the research mission statement and strategic plan to facilitate a practice-wide discussion to examine practical implications, and transformational potential, of committing to research. Effective sessions will define practice-based research through examples from architectural practice to inform discussion; demonstrate support for research in principle by senior managers with responsibility for practice management; integrate perspectives from architectural support staff and existing consultants to gain an appreciation of areas of potential interest; gauge willingness to participate in research practice and assess existing capacity within the practice. It may be time-effective to invite an experienced practitioner-researcher familiar with architectural practice to facilitate practice workshops to explain the potential of practice-based research, capture consensus or dissent about the potential scope of the research programme, and interpret staff feedback and generate cost-effective strategies for the practice to move forward with a shared purpose.

Acknowledgements

The chapter draws on the author's direct experiences of leading Metropolitan Workshop's A New Kind of Suburbia (2019–21). I would like to thank Neil Deely, Tom Mitchell, Jonny McKenna, Gareth Bansor, Kruti Patel, Richard Robinson and all colleagues who contributed to the practice's first extended research project. Special thanks are due to Dr Elanor Warwick (Clarion Housing Group) for her guidance during the later phases of analysis, and Ava Lynam (Metropolitan Workshop and Technische Universität Berlin) for sharing her reflections on conducting practice-based research, which have informed the focus of this chapter.

1 KA Martindale, *Research for Architectural Practice*, Abingdon, Routledge, 2022; R Lucas, *Research Methods for Architecture*, London, Laurence King Publishing, 2016, pp 59–68; F Samuel, *Why Architects Matter: Evidencing and Communicating the Value of Architects*, Abingdon, Routledge, 2018, pp 191–200; A Akšamija, *Research Methods for the Architectural Profession*, New York, Routledge, 2021; L Groat and D Wang, *Architectural Research Methods*, Hoboken, NJ, John Wiley & Sons, 2013.
Several accessible guides are available to guide architects undertaking practice-based research, and provide informative cases aligned to a range of disciplinary perspectives. Martindale offers comprehensive advice including the development of research proposals, handling research ethics, gaining research funding, implementing research processes, and disseminating research in academic and practice contexts. Ray provides a highly accessible introduction to a variety of research methods, including a discussion of productive frameworks for cross-disciplinary collaboration. Samuel outlines models of academic and practice collaboration. Akšamija summarises differences between pursuing a research career in industry and academia, maps research processes against the architectural design process to support project-based research, and gives guidance on the integration of research into architectural practice.

2 A Yaneva, *Made by the Office for Metropolitan Architecture: An Ethnography of Design*, Rotterdam, 010 Publishers, 2009; T Yarrow, *Architects: Portraits of a Practice*, Ithaca, NY, Cornell University Press, 2019. Yaneva and Yarrow offer valuable, recent insight into social realities of architectural practice, from the perspectives of academic researchers conducting research within practice as outsider-researchers.

3 F Samuel, 'Supporting research in practice', *The Journal of Architecture*, vol. 22, no. 1, 2017, pp 4–10, https://doi.org/10.1080/13602365.2017.1280288.

4 F Duffy and L Hutton, *Architectural Knowledge: The Idea of a Profession*, London, E&FN Spon, 1998; R Hay, N Shasore and F Samuel, 'Research at the RIBA: An institutional history 1958–1971', *Architectural Research Quarterly*, vol. 21, no. 4, 2017, pp 328–37, https://doi.org/10.1017/S135913551800012X; Akšamija, *Research Methods for the Architectural Profession*, pp 26–7. At the time of writing, the Royal Institute of British Architects (RIBA), American Institute of Architects (AIA) and Architectural Institute of Japan (AIJ) offered examples of professional bodies with well-developed strategies for promoting research by architects and practitioners within extended fields of architecture.

5 Martindale, *Research for Architectural Practice*, pp 3–34.

6 D Saunt, T Greenall and R Marcaccio, eds, *The Business of Research: Knowledge and Learning Redefined in Architectural Practice*, Chichester, John Wiley & Sons, 2019.

7 A Dye and F Samuel, eds, *Demystifying Architectural Research: Adding Value to Your Practice*, London, RIBA Publishing, 2015; Martindale, *Research for Architectural Practice*, pp 121–237; RIBA, *Research in Practice Guide*, London, RIBA, 2013, https://www.architecture.com/-/media/gathercontent/home-improvements-housing-research-in-practice/additional-documents/ribaresearchinpracticeguidepdf (accessed 4 March 2022); RIBA, *How Architects Use Research: Case Studies from Practice*, London, RIBA, 2014, https://www.architecture.com/knowledge-and-resources/resources-landing-page/how-architects-use-research (accessed 4 March 2022); RIBA, President's Awards for Research 2016: Knowledge and Research Practice, London, RIBA, 2016, https://www.architecture.com/knowledge-and-resources/resources-landing-page/knowledge-and-research-in-practice (accessed 4 March 2022).

8 Samuel, *Why Architects Matter*, pp 201–4.

9 K Firth, 'A fruitful coupling', *Urban Design Group Journal*, no. 157, 2021, pp 18–22, https://www.udg.org.uk/publications/journal/urban-design-157-winter-2021 (accessed 4 March 2022).

10 J Dean, *Doing Reflexivity: An Introduction*, Bristol, Polity

Press, 2017; P Drake and L Heath, *Practitioner Research at Doctoral Level: Developing Coherent Research Methodologies*, Abingdon, Routledge, 2011; M Alvesson and K Skoldberg, *Reflexive Methodology: New Vistas for Qualitative Research*, London, SAGE Publications, 2000. The value for research quality of researchers 'becoming reflective/reflexive' is well established in qualitative research, whether conducted in practice or academia.

11 Samuel, Why Architects Matter, p 2; Lucas, *Research Methods for Architecture, pp* 59–68.

12 N Deely, 'Introduction', in L Mallett, ed., *People Make Places Make People: 12 Year Anniversary Book*, London, Metropolitan Workshop, 2017, p4.

13 DA Sookhoo, 'Reflections on a new kind of suburbia', *Urban Design Group Journal*, no. 157, 2021, pp 23–6, https://www.udg.org.uk/publications/journal/urban-design-157-winter-2021 (accessed 4 March 2022); J McKenna, 'The Homestead: The basic building block of a new type of suburbia', in *RIAI Journal*, no. 308, November/December 2019, p 35.
The Homestead is a typological device that aims to structure new types of suburban development that are efficient in form, respond to changing market conditions through flexible densities, typologies and tenure mixes, and are capable of optimising private and public space to enhance the public realm for greater sociability.

14 DA Sookhoo, N Deely and G Bansor, eds, *A New Kind of Suburbia (Prospects 1)*, London, Metropolitan Workshop, 2019. External practice contributors included Dinah Bornat (ZCD Architects), Mark Latham (Urban Splash), Jo McCafferty (Levitt Bernstein), Richard Partington (Studio Partington) and Toby Carr (Sarah Wigglesworth Architects).

15 DA Sookhoo, 'Suburbia making architects', in Sookhoo, Deely and Bansor, eds, *A New Kind of Suburbia*, pp 51–61; T Mitchell, 'Building community through play: Discussing the legacy and lessons of the provision of informal and planned playspaces and sports facilities in Crawley New Town', 4 November 2021, https://metwork.co.uk/research/people-powered-places (accessed 4 April 2022); N Deely, 'Semi-detached', in D Levitt and J McCafferty, eds, *The Housing Handbook: A Good Practice Guide*, London, Routledge, 2019, pp 20–1. Practice members were invited to produce auto-ethnographic accounts to reflect on how their formative experiences as suburban residents informed their aspirations for the suburban places they created in their professional work (e.g., the desire to create opportunities for community through play).

16 J McKenna, D Murray and DA Sookhoo, eds, *A New Kind of Suburbia (Prospects 1 – Dublin Version)*, Dublin, Metropolitan Workshop, pp 2–4.

17 DA Sookhoo, E Warwick and N Deely, eds, *A New Kind of Suburbia: Reflections for Future Practice and Thinking: Record of Exhibition Talks, Roundtable Findings and Practice Recommendations*, London, Metropolitan Workshop, 2021, p1. The London exhibition contributed to the Clerkenwell Design Week and London Festival of Architecture, and the Dublin exhibition contributed to the Irish Architecture Foundation's 2019 Open House Dublin.

18 Sookhoo, Warwick and N Deely, eds, *A New Kind of Suburbia*, pp 3–13. Exhibition talks were delivered by David Birkbeck (Design for Homes), Peter Freeman (Argent), Mark Latham (Urban Splash), Gus Zogolovitch (Unboxed Homes), John O'Mahony (O'Mahony Architects), Michael Pike (GKMP), Joe Brady (School of Geography, UCD), Eddie Conroy (South Dublin County Council) and Brian Moran (Hines).

19 DA Sookhoo and E Warwick, 'Future suburban practice, future suburban places', in Sookhoo, Warwick and Deely, eds, *A New Kind of Suburbia*, pp 14–23. Roundtable participants included Elanor Warwick (Clarion), Andy von Bradsky (then, MHCLG), Keith Brown (then, community organiser, Nationwide Building Society), Graham Cherry (Countryside), Vincent Lacovara (Enfield Council), Chris Langdon (ENGIE), Stephen Proctor (Proctor Matthews Architects), Mark Swenarton (Liverpool University), Sarah Wigglesworth (SWA), Dhruv Sookhoo (then, Metropolitan Workshop) and Neil Deely (Metropolitan Workshop).

20 DA Sookhoo, E Warwick and N Deely, 'Recommendations for future practice (and research) for suburban development', in Metropolitan Workshop, *A New Kind of Suburbia: The Takeaway*, London, Metropolitan Workshop, 2021.

21 Metropolitan Workshop, 'A new kind of suburbia', *Metropolitan Workshop*, 1 November 2021, Research, https://metwork.co.uk/research/a-new-kind-of-suburbia/ (accessed 4 March 2022).

22 Ibid.

23 Sookhoo, 'Reflections on a new kind of suburbia'.

24 Universities apply a standard approach to costing research projects based on decades of experience of bidding for funds competitively, and delivering projects within academic settings with established specialist labour costs for researchers, shared access to academic managers with an understanding of research and dissemination processes, and efficiencies arising from the routine research procedures and processes. It is reasonable to assume that architectural practices undertaking a research project for the first time will be less efficient as they develop approaches that are cost-effective, flexibly delivered and achieve research quality, in relation to the constraints and opportunities measured by practice management processes.

25 Martindale, *Research for Architectural Practice*, pp 109–20. Martindale offers detailed guidance on the dissemination of research through self-publication and peer-reviewed books, academic journals, conference papers and exhibitions.

26 M Latham and DA Sookhoo, 'New suburbia, now: The possibilities of modular construction', *Architectural Research Quarterly,* vol. 23, no. 2, 2019, pp 195–200, https://doi.org/10.1017/S1359135519000253; D Prichard and DA Sookhoo, 'Recalling Milton Keynes: Visions of suburbia', *Architectural Research Quarterly,* vol. 23, no. 3, 2019, pp 288–95, https://doi.org/10.1017/S1359135519000344; Sookhoo, 'Reflections on a new kind of suburbia'; DA Sookhoo and A Ely, 'Fundamentals of creating local identity', session presented to Code School, Urban Design London, virtual, 7 May–8 July 2021; DA Sookhoo and K Patel, 'Oakfield Village. A healthier kind of suburb', guest lecture presented to Masters of Urban Design, Newcastle University, Newcastle upon Tyne, 25 November 2021; A Odedun, 'Places, spaces and sociality', People, Places and Community: belonging in unprecedented time (Future of London), blog post, 9 December 2021, https://www.futureoflondon.org.uk/knowledge/people-place-community/ (accessed 4 April 2022); J McKenna and DA Sookhoo, interview with R O'Ceallaigh, 'A new kind of suburbia: Practice-based research', podcast, *Green Urbanist*, 29 March 2021, https://greenurbanistpod.com/ (accessed 4 April 2022). See Metropolitan Workshop, 'A new kind of suburbia' for full list of outputs.

27 Akšamija, *Research Methods for the Architectural Profession*, pp 20–9.

28 R Cowan, *Essential Urban Design: A Handbook for Architects, Designers and Planners*, London: RIBA Publishing, 2021, p 187; T Townshend, *Healthy Cities? Design for Wellbeing*, London, Lund Humphries, 2022, pp 82–4.

29 Sookhoo, 'Reflections on a new kind of suburbia', p 26.

30 B Macfarlane, E Devine, T Drake, A Gilbert, M Robinson and I White, *'Co-authorship in humanities and the social sciences: A global view', white paper,* 2017, pp 8–10, https://authorservices.taylorandfrancis.com/wp-content/uploads/2017/09/Coauthorship-white-paper.pdf (accessed 4 March 2022). Co-authorship is earned by being responsible for the conception and design of a research project, analysis and interpretation of data, drafting the paper and revisiting it critically for intellectual content or, potentially, approval of the final version to be published. There is limited consensus on the order that authors' names should appear, but a good rule of thumb is to consider how essential each author was to the activities listed above, and order from the most critical to the least critical.

31 Akšamija, *Research Methods for the Architectural Profession*, pp 24–9. An effective *research agenda* will reflect the practice's structure, and interests in specific markets, building types or areas of expertise to be examined or expanded through research. Developing a *research agenda* may act as an intermediate stage between preparing a *mission statement* and a *strategic plan.*

32 Martindale, *Research for Architectural Practice*, pp 58–65. Martindale offers detailed guidance on the preparation of research proposals for architectural research.

33 Samuel, 'Supporting research in practice', p 8.

34 K Scalon, F Blanc, J Drage, C Reid and J Cook, *A Portrait of Aspirant Homeowners in London: LSE London Report with Pocket Living and Metropolitan Workshop*, London, London School of Economics, 2020, https://blogsmedia.lse.ac.uk/blogs.dir/119/files/2020/07/Final-Report-LSE-London-MW-and-Pocket-Living-Research-2020.pdf (accessed 4 March 2022); J Drage, DA Sookhoo and N Deely, 'Case study: Mapleton Crescent, Wandsworth, London', in S Bayliss and S and R Bergin, eds, *The Modular Housing Handbook*, Newcastle upon Tyne, RIBA Publishing, 2020, pp 183–92.

Co-design Tools: Regenerating Communities

Kyle Buchanan and Sarah Ahmed, Archio

Left: Mellis Haward of Archio facilitating a co-design session with members of Greenwich Citizens Housing. The workshops went beyond answering site-specific questions, and gave the community group the power to determine which future sites might be suitable for their affordable housing aims, providing them with transferable skills to inform their campaign.

Opposite: A collective rehearsal: Archio co-design workshop in Lewisham. The whole studio relocated to a garage site to run a three-day co-design workshop with neighbouring residents. Local people were trained to use the foam cutter and other modelling tools, to become active participants in the design process and engage with the complexities of infill site development.

There is a prevailing narrative in our industry of the architect losing influence;[1] at its heart is a characterisation of a lone genius solving the intractable problems of our cities and societies with the sheer brilliance of their mind. The reality is that the social and political context architects find themselves working in today is woven with challenges that are simply too big and complex to be solved by a single bright idea. We are due a reframing of how architects practise, moving away from the heroic and towards a new role as facilitators, advocates and unpackers of complex problems.

The first part of this chapter explores the case for using co-design to build more effective collaborations with communities, so that they are better represented in regeneration. The second section draws on our experience of working with community groups to set out co-design tools and tips that can be applied in practice. We conclude that co-design approaches have the potential to deliver long-term benefit by upskilling communities and empowering them to participate more widely, delivering more equitable outcomes as a result.

The case for co-design in regeneration

Regeneration, the term used to describe the active promotion of economic growth in cities and towns, aims to deliver prosperity through strategic planning and investment mainly in the form of new buildings and infrastructure. Whether successful or not, regeneration is always a byword for change. This change is most obviously physical; however, spatial interventions are often accompanied by economic and social changes. An improved urban environment tends to mean a more valuable one: rents and property prices rise, putting pressure on existing residents and businesses, who frequently find themselves 'priced out'.

With a staggering 14.5 million people in the UK living in poverty,[2] there is an urgent need for investment in housing and social infrastructure; however, growth does not always mean change in the right direction. The emphasis on economic growth as a universal solution to environmental and societal challenges can be detrimental to the complex social networks that hold together existing communities.

There is certainly an initial fear among many existing resident communities that regeneration is something done to them, rather than with them or for their benefit. Put another way, the change that accompanies regeneration brings winners and losers. The losers are often people who were in a more precarious position to start with, people who don't own their homes, or those whose business model relies on low rents and the concentration of other similar businesses these can attract. This ultimately results in opposition to regeneration, creating a situation which is bad for everyone – regeneration becomes more difficult to deliver because of local opposition, and local people miss out on the opportunity to benefit from the right sort of investment that well-delivered urban renewal can bring.

Ultimately, who should benefit from regeneration is a political question. We take the position that where public investment is required, there is an obligation to see the benefits of that investment spread as widely as possible, and particularly within existing communities. Edward Glaeser says that 'because the essential characteristic of humanity is our ability to learn from each other, cities make us more human',[3] and certainly communities that have built up organically and slowly over time have a texture and richness that is difficult to replicate with quick-fix meanwhile uses.

There are many benefits to living in a functioning community, including to mental and physical health, and existing communities should be seen as a scarce resource to be cherished amid change.

In her essay 'In it together', architect, educator and writer Lesley Lokko says that 'in coming together, we rehearse a collective script that's been around for centuries: the script of the city, the play of urban life'.[4] This description of city making as 'rehearsing a collective script' is an evocative one, and raises the question of what that rehearsal might look like. It reminds us of the co-design that we use with community-led housing groups and others, and perhaps offers a clue to a more inclusive approach that can give existing communities a greater stake in regeneration.

Left: Block modelling at Brasted Close, Lewisham. Using a foam cutter is a quick way to model blocks and massing, and this method enabled local people to engage with the complexities of development on this tricky site.

Below: A flow chart, produced by Archio, setting out how and when participants can engage in the design process. The flow chart is designed to be visually engaging and easy to understand, enabling participants to see how and when they will be involved, as the project progresses in complexity and decisions are fixed.

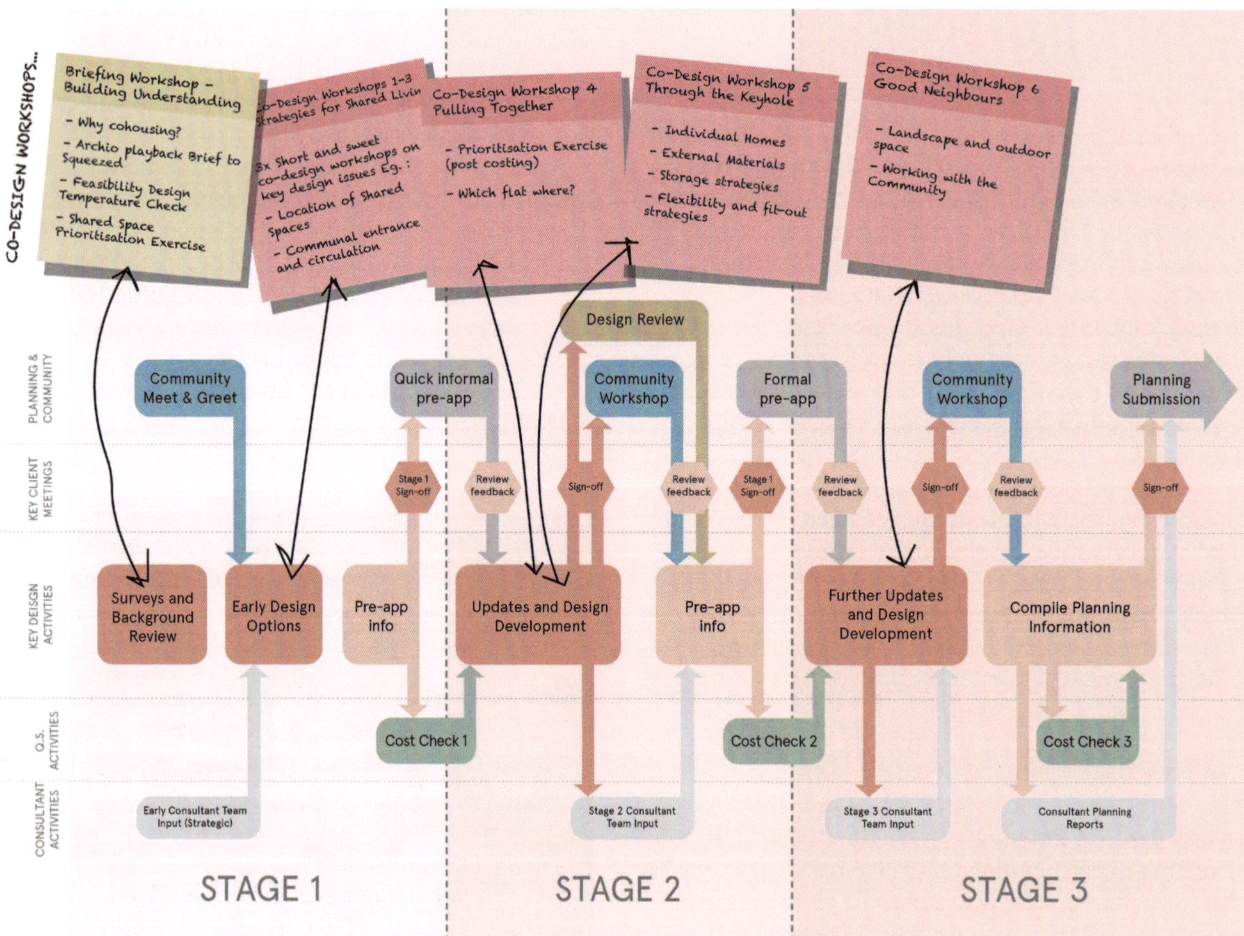

It is often suggested that good design comes from listening to users' needs,[5] which, in the context of city making, assumes that existing communities will have the inclination, expertise and time to come forward and share their thoughts with a design team. When we talk about co-design, we have in mind an altogether more active approach. Co-design can take many forms, but its success depends on collaboration – on a two-way flow of information between designer and user. The architect brings to the table expert knowledge, while the user brings history and lived experience, each of which is given equal significance.

Community-led housing, in which regeneration is literally led by the community, is a fertile ground for co-design but it has wider potential as well. If anything, the lesser the involvement of an existing community the greater the case for engaging them through co-design. This is a responsibility that falls to architects, design teams and their commissioning clients – who have a professional and, we would suggest, moral obligation to deliver public benefit through regeneration. Fragile and intangible social networks are easily shattered by the wrong approach, and it is all too easy for architects to be complicit in disempowering residents.

If design is a problem-solving exercise, then co-design's aim should be to frame the problem in a way in which marginalised members of the community can voice their needs in a productive setting. As Jeremy Till says, 'the key [to co-design] lies in recognising the power and validity of ordinary conversation'[6] to transform the architect's knowledge into something that might be more democratically employed.

Our own experience has been that engaging in this 'ordinary conversation' with local residents can have transformative results. One of our first co-designed housing projects, Brasted Close Community Land Trust in Lewisham, received 107 letters of support at planning – and support at that level is surely evidence that with the right approach regeneration can be both popular, and wide reaching in its benefit.

In the next section, we explore some of the co-design approaches and tools that we have used at Brasted Close, and on other projects, in our efforts to deliver regeneration that puts the community front and centre.

Positive regeneration – a co-design toolkit

Archio have been co-designing housing-led regeneration with communities for many years and have developed a 'co-design toolkit' that promotes inclusivity and foregrounds residents' interests. Much of our approach has been developed through work with community-led housing groups, but more recently we have begun using the same tools in new contexts, for example on council-led development. The success in these new sectors has demonstrated the potential for this approach to enrich the regeneration process more generally.

In the section below we set out four key strategies that we use when co-designing with communities: 'giving other people the pen', 'establishing representative and constructive conversations', 'facilitating decision-making' and 'empowering communities long term', providing specific examples of tools that we use to achieve these.

1. Giving other people the pen

Co-design has so much potential for success because it enables non-expert lived experiences to inform design outcomes, which we describe as 'giving other people the pen'. This can be done through workshops that use simple tools like block models, or online platforms such as Miro, which require limited training and allow people to influence designs in real time. Allowing others into the process does not dimmish the need for architects' design skills and, if anything, greater agility is required to guide and coach participants.

Residents need to be involved early, ideally before any design work has begun. Developing a design before residents have had a chance to communicate their views and experience makes it less likely that it will address their needs and risks creating the impression that participants are simply being asked to validate a pre-decided outcome.

Design processes can be disorienting for the uninitiated, and not knowing when or how you are able to influence a design is stressful and confusing. Members of the public will not usually have previous design experience and may be contributing voluntarily in their spare time. Setting out a clear process of what should be expected at each stage encourages more constructive and extensive engagement. We use simple flow charts to show how co-design workshops fit into overall design development, enabling participants to understand the points at which they are expected to contribute and the influence their contributions will have.

The need to make design accessible extends to how co-design workshops and other events are structured. We find it useful to share workshop plans in advance, so participants know what to expect. We begin each session by recapping key learnings from the last meeting and setting out expected outcomes from

CO-DESIGN TIP
The power of the Post-it note

The humble Post-it note becomes a powerful tool in the context of a co-design workshop. Its smallness and familiarity reassure participants, encouraging them to make contributions. Complex ideas can be built up and articulated in a colourful jigsaw of simple statements and ideas.

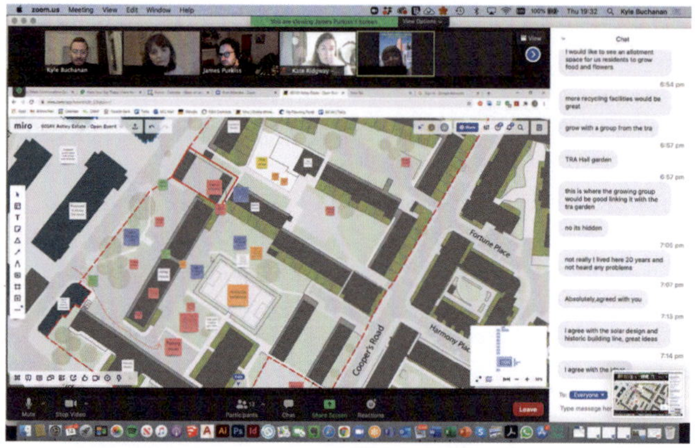

Above: An online co-design session, run by Archio, using an experience-mapping exercise with residents in Southwark was used to draw out stories and experiential anecdotes about the housing estate. Taking the time to understand how people really live and experience the place directly informed the estate improvements proposed as part of this housing-led regeneration scheme.

Below: Archio's public exhibition boards at The Phoenix, Lewes, seeking feedback on co-housing proposals. The Post-it note is a familiar tool that, unlike a questionnaire, invites participants to engage with everyone else's commentary and feedback, building up layers of conversation.

the current one. During the workshop we facilitate contributions by asking questions and using other techniques such as thought experiments to make sure conversations remain focused. It is important to help everyone attending to contribute – some people will naturally be more comfortable doing so than others, and it may be necessary to draw quieter members of a group into conversation directly. Setting up patterns around how workshops are run means that participants become familiar with the format and feel more comfortable engaging.

2. Establishing representative and constructive conversations

A co-design group needs a broad and representative range of voices if it is to reflect the needs of the wider community. Determining the appropriate mix of a group means first understanding the demographic make-up of an area. This requires a systematic approach – at Brasted Close, we used desktop research to understand the community around the site, supplemented by surveys sent to churches, schools and different subcommunities.

It is often the case that creating a representative co-design group can require a degree of curation. There are elements of any community who will be less inclined to engage in regeneration processes, and efforts must be made to encourage these 'harder to reach' constituents into discussions. One of the most effective ways to do this is through organisations that have existing connections with groups you are trying to reach. While we were working on a project in Southwark, it became clear that young people were not attending workshops and were therefore under-represented in discussions. To address this, we contacted the charity Southwark Young Advisors,[7] working with 16- to 24-year-olds to engage them in decision-making and service improvements, and they were able to encourage more young people to contribute to our co-design process.

Demonstrating that you understand and can empathise with a community is an effective way to build trust, which is an important part of establishing an effective dialogue. This is aided by having a design team with diverse backgrounds who can bring their own experience to discussions, provide cultural insights and connect with participants through shared life experiences.

Similarly, the space in which co-design workshops take place impacts how comfortable people feel. Running in-person workshops in community spaces close to a development site means that people don't have to travel to take part and are put at ease by being on familiar ground. Digital sessions have the advantage that people don't need to travel at all and can access events from their own homes; however, communication can be more challenging. We have recently been trialling hybrid sessions, which offer maximum flexibility by giving people the choice of attending in person or virtually.

In either context, the language of communication is important. Technical jargon and traditional ways of representing designs can be alienating to non-expert participants, creating unintentional barriers. Using simple language to explain best-practice approaches helps demystify design and enables people without formal design training to contribute valuable insights.

The approaches above are important to establish trust; however, this needs to be translated into rapport if an effective working relationship is to be developed between designers and community participants. One of the ways we build rapport in the early stages of a project is through 'ice-breaker' exercises, which help us get to know groups and to start conversation in a non-pressured way. One of our favourites is the 'hopes and fears' exercise, in which we ask participants to use Post-it notes to write down their hopes or fears around a project. This gives people a chance to reflect and share their individual experiences without having to take a definitive position on any particular point. By the end of the session the Post-it notes create a record of priorities, which can offer invaluable clues to the design team as the process progresses.

A 'hopes and fears' exercise, run by Archio, using colourful Post-it notes to begin the co-design process. Asking people their greatest hope and scariest fear for a project helps to unveil the true reason behind somebody's 'position' and can provide input into the overarching vision for a project.

Left: Open questions give a voice to all members of a community group to communicate their ambitions. While someone might feel inhibited giving feedback on a design point or technical query, open questions that are more qualitative can be engaging to a wider audience.

Below: A 'temperature check' exercise run by Archio with a co-housing group in Norwich, showing individual members' preferences and giving shape to shared group ambitions. The exercise allows a broad position to be chosen, without requiring participants to be definitive in their answers.

CO-DESIGN TIP
Ask open questions

Asking open questions (questions that cannot be answered by a simple 'yes' or 'no') gives people the space and freedom to explore possibilities and express their concerns. Allowing participants to speak openly often draws out important insights that might not have been considered previously.

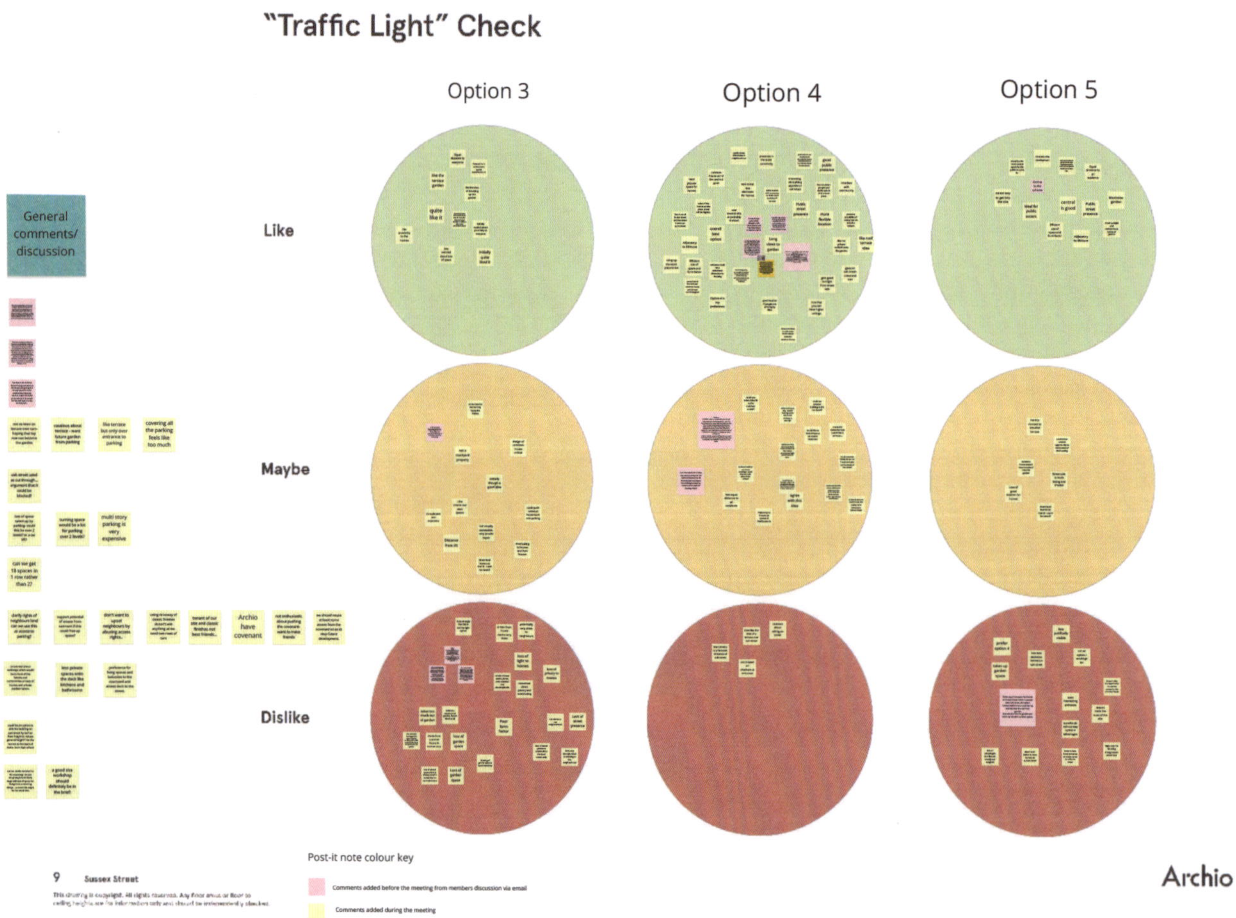

3. Facilitating decision-making

Conventional approaches to decision-making are generally either autocratic, where a leader or leadership group makes decisions that others follow, or democratic, where the majority decide the course of action. In co-design the risk of these approaches is that group members who do not agree with a decision can feel marginalised. This can result in a loss of cohesion, with people who feel excluded either leaving the group or otherwise disrupting progress. We have found that a sociocratic approach to decision-making, which aims to achieve a consensus, is a more a productive approach.

Where consensus is reached quickly this is straightforward, but this is not always the case. A large part the role of the architect-as-facilitator is supporting groups to make decisions everyone can buy into – a task that becomes harder to achieve the larger the group.

Tools such as temperature checks and traffic lighting are useful because they stop short of asking people to give definitive answers. In these exercises participants are asked to commit a single vote to one of three feelings (e.g., like, maybe or dislike) to give both architects and participants an indication of where momentum lies.

The emphasis is on identifying areas of common ground and finding solutions where there are areas of difference, so that by the end of a process people are aligned in support. This is done through discussing design options and through thought experiments – 'would you feel comfortable letting your children play in the space unattended?' – and so on. It is important to try to avoid forcing a decision, as this risks ignoring important points of difference. Where we have broad consensus on an issue, but some points of difference remain, we tend to note these for discussion in the future so that what has been agreed can be banked and the process can move forward.

Voting with their feet: a consensus ladder identifies shared ambition by participants standing in different marked zones. In collaboration with TOWN developers, Archio ran this exercise to enable members of the co-housing group to understand each other's standpoint, without asking for a definitive 'vote'.

CO-DESIGN TIP
Give shape to shared ambition

Understanding the underlying interest behind people's stated position (what is really driving their comments) helps to give a clearer sense of concerns and what a mutually acceptable solution might look like. Understanding the 'why' helps dovetail solutions to other people's concerns to achieve consensus.

4. Empowering communities long term

Being able to actively contribute to design decisions can upskill participants with knowledge that outlives the design of a single project, and which can continue to deliver future benefits.

The designer-facilitator should actively seek opportunities to share knowledge and expertise, and to train participants through the process. There is benefit in providing community groups with workshop templates for their own use, and we have had feedback from community-led housing groups that the tools and approaches we have introduced have later been valuable in their own decision-making. One co-housing group in Norwich now uses a temperature check to reach consensus during its own meetings.

Co-design can act as a platform for community cohesion. At Brasted Close our co-design process was supported throughout by Lewisham Citizens, a community organising charity that had initiated the project; their input was invaluable in encouraging a broad spectrum of local communities into the conversation. They contacted local community groups, raising awareness and advocating for the new affordable homes, bringing people together for broader discussions at regular monthly meetings and on-site social events. The Citizens' events ran in parallel to our co-design workshops, with the development project providing

Residents and community organisers at Brasted Close come together to reflect on what the new housing will mean for the community. Many neighbours of the site met for the first time through the co-design process run by Archio.

a focal point for wider discussions about community building. More than one local resident told us they had met their neighbours for the first time at either a design or social event, and that doing so had given them a greater sense of being part of a community. That sense of community, the potential to work together to deliver positive change, is ultimately what co-design brings to regeneration.

Regeneration is about people

Ultimately, good regeneration focuses on people. Prioritising existing communities and making sure they are treated as key collaborators delivers more lasting and equitable results and can help smooth the process along the way.

As architects we need to be brave and let people into the process, and show them that regeneration is something that can be done with them rather than to them. Co-design is a powerful way to do this and allows us to combine our professional expertise with local people's lived experience and insight, delivering projects that are tailored to the priorities and challenges of a particular place. Co-design makes regeneration accessible and demystifies a sometimes-arcane process, giving members of the public confidence that their opinions and experiences are worth hearing and that they have a stake in the future of the places they call home.

Bring social value benefits along the way

Look for opportunities to upskill, inform and even train residents through the regeneration process. You are aiming to leave a legacy of people who are advocates for the change, not just help an individual project to happen.

1 Alan Dunlop, 'The profession is not blameless in its loss of power', *Architectural Journal*, 19 May 2015, https://www.architectsjournal.co.uk/news/opinion/the-profession-is-not-blameless-in-its-loss-of-power, (accessed 25 May 2022).
2 Brigid Francis-Devine, 'Poverty in the UK: Statistics', *House of Commons Library*, 13 April 2022, https://commonslibrary.parliament.uk/research-briefings/sn07096/ (accessed 25 May 2022).
3 Ed Glaeser, The Triumph of the City, Oxford, Pan Macmillan, 2011.
4 Leslie Lokko, 'In it together' in *The Just City Essays: 26 Visions of Inclusion, Equity and Opportunity*, New York, The J Max Bond Center, 2015.
5 'Walk a mile in their shoes', *RIBA Journal*, 1 September 2015, https://www.ribaj.com/intelligence/listening-understanding-clients, (accessed 25 May 2022).
6 Jeremy Till, 'The negotiation of hope', in *Architecture and Participation*, London, Spon Press, 2005.
7 https://youngadvisors.org.uk/southwark/

Getting to Grips with Embodied Carbon

The Making of FCBS Carbon

Dr Joe Jack Williams,
Feilden Clegg Bradley Studios

Over the 40-plus years of Feilden Clegg Bradley Studios, we have been concerned about the impact of our buildings on the wider environment; a practice born out of the oil crisis of the 1970s and embracing the new wave of sustainability in the years that followed. Over successive decades the evidence of global warming has become irrefutable, and the window to avoid catastrophic climate change has dwindled significantly. Out of this urgency the Architects Declare movement was created, with the 17 Stirling Prize-winning UK architects signing up to an 11-point declaration that bound them to reducing the impact of the built environment. Since May 2019, over 1,200 architectural practices have signed up, with the declaration being repeated across other sectors of the built environment and in other countries.

Accelerate the shift to low embodied carbon materials in all our work.
UK Architects Declare Climate and Biodiversity Emergency[1]

As an industry, our focus has predominantly been on low operational energy design but, with the decarbonising electricity grid in the UK, the carbon impact of our buildings has now shifted towards embodied carbon. Within the 11 Architects Declare points this was recognised, with a number of statements relating to embodied and whole-life carbon, which at the time was an emerging field. In the industry there was little knowledge about embodied carbon, and little intuition of how to design and construct a low embodied carbon building.

At FCBStudios we were lucky enough to have some knowledge on whole-life carbon from previous doctoral research, although it had only been used on a small number of studies. As a founding signatory of Architects Declare, the studio felt it had to lead by example, actively engaging with the embodied carbon footprint of projects from the outset. The biggest impacts on a project's footprint could be made at the initial design stages, when the massing is malleable and the underlying brief can be robustly interrogated. But, as a practice, we had no way of assessing and guiding our projects towards the lowest-carbon solution. It was out of this need that we developed what would become FCBS CARBON, our whole-life carbon tool.

FCBS CARBON had three key intentions:

- Measure the impact of early design decisions.
- Record the whole-life carbon impact of our projects
- Educate the practice on whole-life carbon thinking.

Through the use of FCBS CARBON, the intention was to not only measure and record the whole-life carbon of our projects, but also to support the design process, highlighting the impact of design changes on carbon emissions. This active use of FCBS CARBON is an engaging way for the design team to learn about how the built environment causes carbon emissions, filling the knowledge gap around embodied carbon.

A key barrier to estimating embodied carbon at those early design stages is establishing a bill of materials (BoM). Creating a BoM is time-consuming, and requires

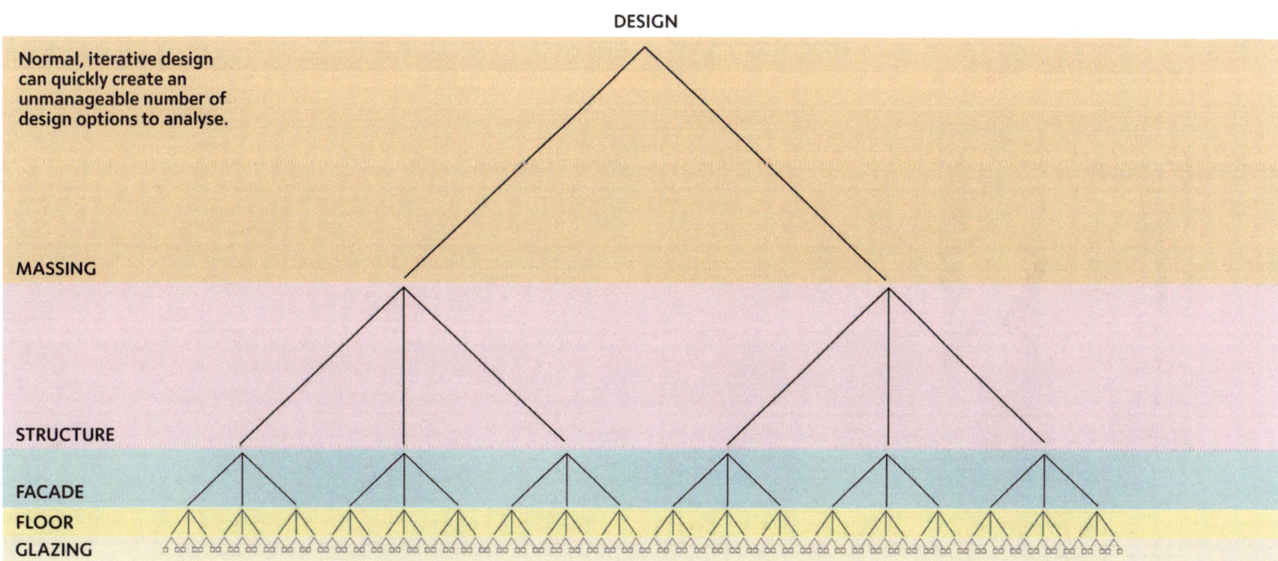

Right: Data is inputted to FCBS CARBON within an Excel sheet, producing easy-to-read graphs. These show the distribution of embodied carbon of the new building, by building aspect, and how the design scores on the RIBA 2030 Challenge scale.

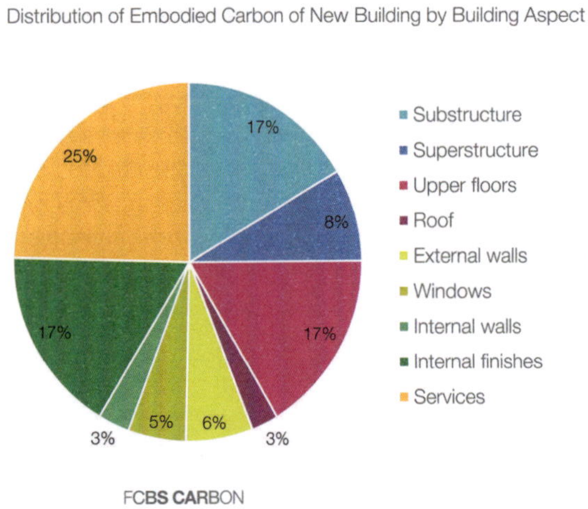

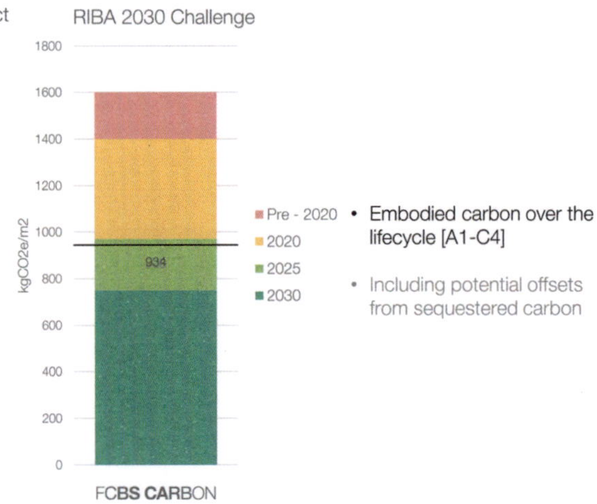

Below: From the data inputted to FCBS CARBON, a series of output graphs are created, showing: a) operational energy use; b) life cycle embodied carbon; c) whole-life carbon; and d) offset carbon.

OPERATIONAL ENERGY

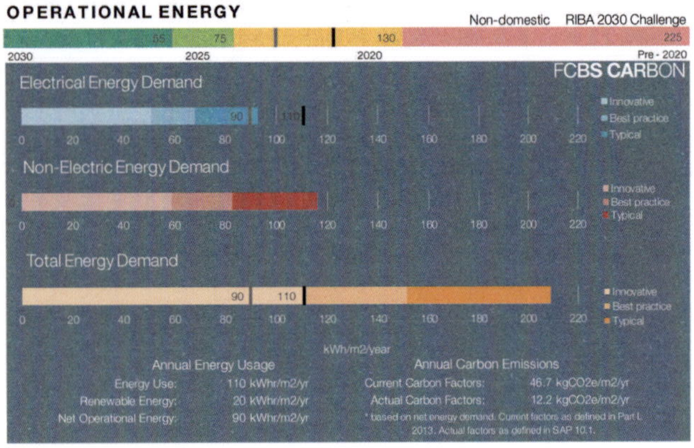

LIFECYCLE EMBODIED CARBON

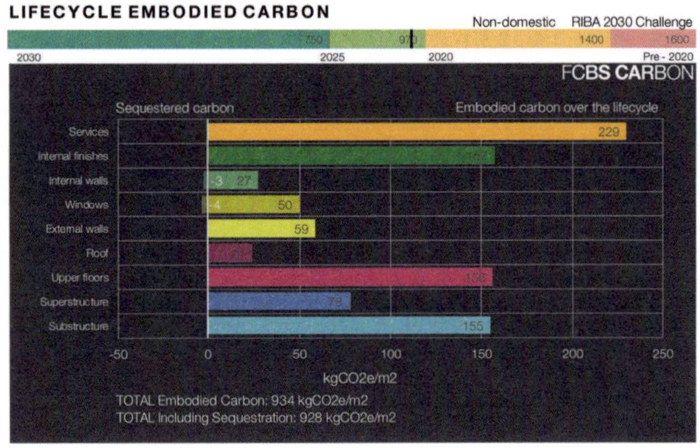

WHOLE LIFE CARBON

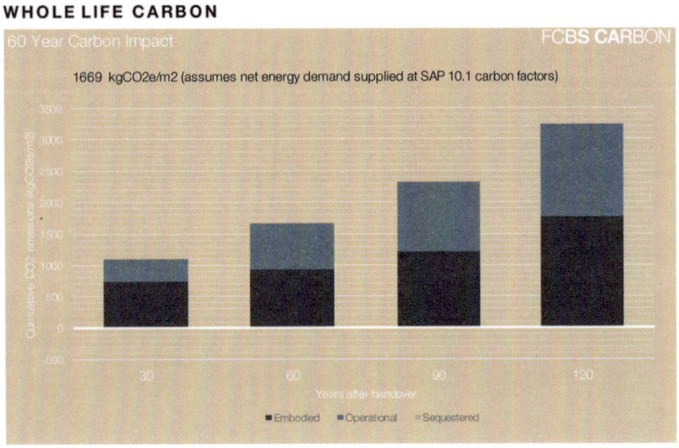

OFFSET CARBON

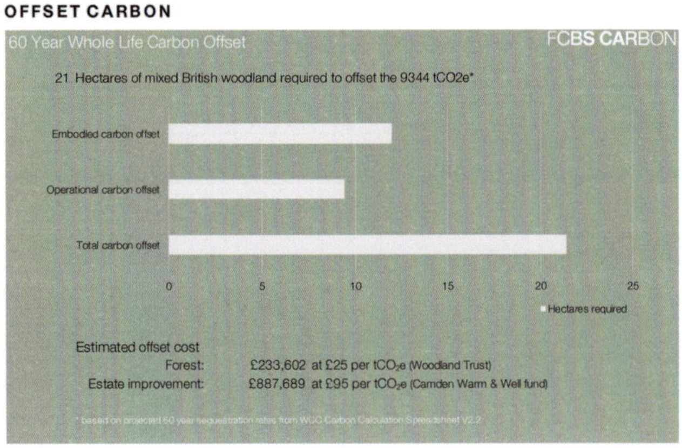

Design for the Translational Office Space Project at the Wellcome Genome Campus in Hinxton, using a glulam and CLT structure.

detailed knowledge of construction and materials, as well as the building form. At these early stages, two different massings could easily lead to as many as 108 different design options, each of which would need a BoM to make an accurate estimate of the embodied carbon. Instead, it's possible to use some basic building parameters to estimate the building quantities, which are then applied to typical construction components. This algorithmic approach approximates the overall embodied carbon of a building, but means that bold changes, such as adding a floor or changing a facade construction, can be quickly assessed for impact. While this provides an approximation of the embodied carbon, the direction and magnitude of the changes are assessed against a consistent method, giving a good indication of the relative impact of design changes.

In-house carbon calculator

Initially, FCBS CARBON was designed as an internal tool, for the teams at FCBStudios to gain knowledge and experience of whole-life and embodied carbon emissions. The components used to create the buildings were based on our typical build-ups, representing the scale and types of projects we work on. A component list was created of typical build-ups, each modelled for embodied carbon emissions using Environmental Product Declaration (EPD) data or generic figures from the Inventory of Carbon and Energy (ICE) V3 database. This simplifies the material choices; choosing ceramic cladding not only models the cladding material, but also the necessary support structure to create that facade, which can itself be a higher emitter than the rainscreen material.

Through use with project teams, we spent time trying to craft the embodied carbon outputs required for them to make informed choices, while giving scale to what could be an unknowable carbon emission figure. With the release of the RIBA 2030 figures in 2019, the industry had the first markers to show what overall emissions figures meant, giving the important context needed for understanding the whole-life embodied carbon figures. These are stored within FCBS CARBON and are shown on each page of the inputs, giving immediate feedback on the design changes. The overall outputs give detailed breakdowns of where the emissions arise, key figures for reporting outputs, and indicative offsetting costs.

One of the first live architectural competition entries in which we used FCBS CARBON was the Translational Office Space Project at the Wellcome Genome Campus in Hinxton, for the European Molecular Biology Laboratory and European Bioinformatics Institute (EMBL-EBI). Sustainability was a key driver for the client body, and presented us with an ideal opportunity to test the tool with a wider audience.

As big changes can occur throughout the programme, modelling at the early design stage gave EMBL-EBI an illustration of the variance resulting from key design decisions, as well as a true representation of what they could expect from performance, and alignment with their aspirations.

INTEGRATED SUSTAINABILITY OPTIONS
EMBODIED CARBON

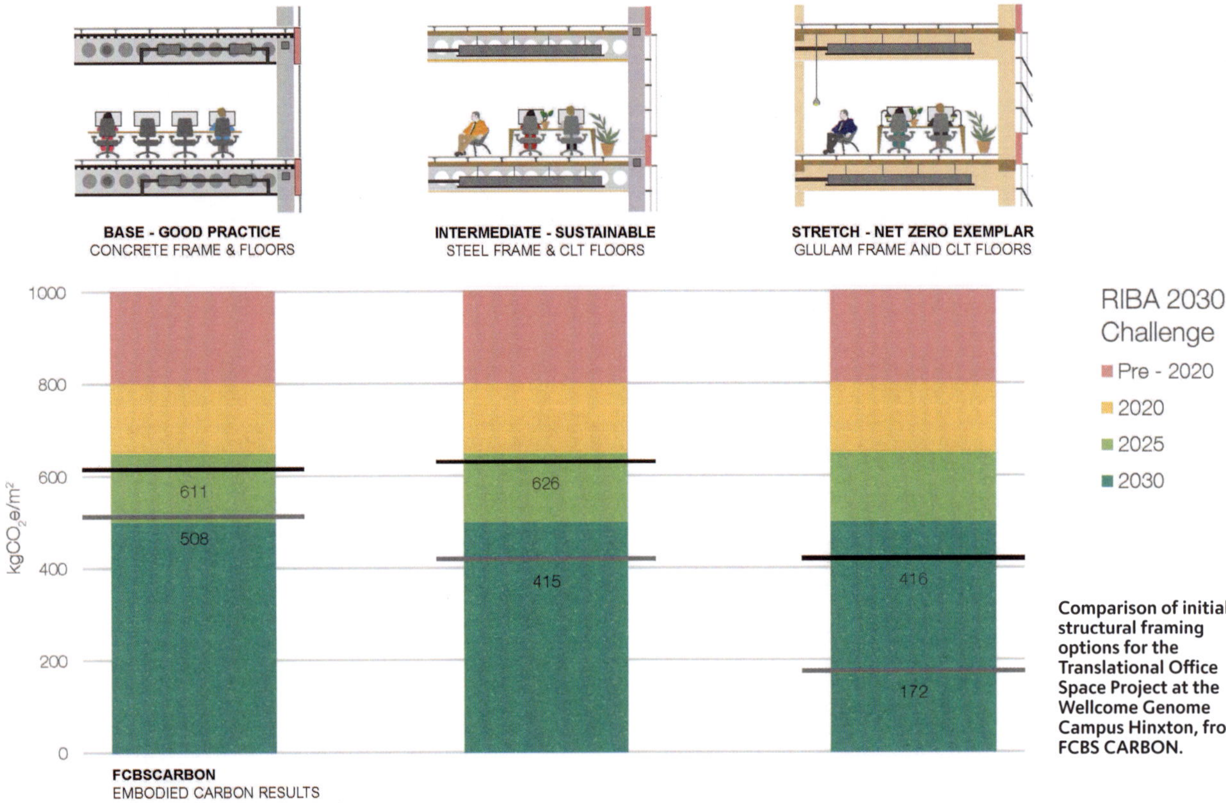

Comparison of initial structural framing options for the Translational Office Space Project at the Wellcome Genome Campus Hinxton, from FCBS CARBON.

This bolstered our push for the extensive use of cross-laminated timber (CLT) and glued laminated timber (glulam) for structure, setting out strong sustainability ambitions from the start and, most importantly, putting a tangible figure on the impact of this design decision.

Knowledge sharing

We realised that our in-house tool filled a niche in the wider industry – and was needed by all in the built environment sector. Reflecting on our Architects Declare commitment to share knowledge, and the urgency of the climate crisis, we realised that this tool should be shared with the wider industry, following other releases such as H\B:ERT by Hawkins\Brown and the Mesh Embodied Carbon Calculator. To move from an in-house tool to one used by the wider industry required additional development, streamlining the data input process and improving the output legibility, but more importantly increasing the robustness of the underlying algorithms and embedded assumptions and approximation methodology. For the architectural elements we were relatively confident in the assumptions, but the structural elements were based only on experience. Given reports on the significant impact of structural elements from guides such as the *LETI Embodied Carbon Primer*[2] and *RICS Whole Life Carbon Assessment for the Built Environment*,[3] we recognised that we had to improve the structural modelling within the tool.

Given the need for accuracy and intelligibility, we assembled a steering group, comprising Simon Sturgis (Targeting Zero), Julia Ratcliffe (Scale Consulting), AKT II and Webb Yates. Each was able to test the early versions of the tool and provide key feedback. Collaborating with this group provided the broader view that we needed to create a useful tool that could support their design processes. Their feedback ranged from informing the underlying structural materials, to finessing the output design to improve legibility. Working with teams from outside architecture gave us a much-needed broader view that strengthened and improved the tool.

Julia Ratcliffe of Scale Consulting (part of our steering group)

Early-stage briefing and design choices leave a permanent legacy on the life cycle impact of a building. I was very keen to help support the development of this tool to inform better decisions from the outset.

FCBStudios' developers engaged early and in an open way about what options to present and how best to develop estimates for the embodied carbon of the frame, in a way appropriate to the level of information that might be available. Next, the adjustment factors came in to allow a wider range of options to be evaluated under an experienced engineering eye – recognising that most sizing would be a function of too many variables to be contained and calculated within the spreadsheet. We were also able to share ideas as well as databases and studies to support methods of estimating both quantities and material carbon data that had been published through engineering institutions, for compatibility with the industry norms and best practice.

It was important that the tool never sought to replace specialist engineering input – but recognised that clients can be unwilling to invest in design, even in these critical design stages. The ability to check sensitivity of the whole-life carbon to these elements, in itself, could convince a client to engage that specialist advice and positively influence the design through strategic influence in brief definition and early concept design activities.

Wider release

In November 2020, the tool was released as an Excel spreadsheet, for free, through the FCBStudios website, and has since been downloaded over 3,500 times. A key part of its success is its format. Using Excel removes the barriers inherent in other software, such as BIM tools, which are not used by all elements of the design team. It also means that this is not a tool just for large design practices, but also small practices, project managers, clients and all those involved in the built environment. Using Excel meant that there were necessary compromises, such as removing macros, to ensure that users could be confident the spreadsheet was safe. This reduced the flexibility, but the increased acceptance was felt to be a fair trade-off to broaden usage and adoption.

Carole Latham of Latham Davies (a small chartered practice and an early adopter of FCBS CARBON)

As a small practice the climate emergency is one we can ably respond to as professionals, but we require a different toolkit to assist in the endeavour. Larger projects and larger practices usually equate to more specialised resources to advise and steer sustainability decision-making. We don't need to be left behind, we can contribute, and we do need the support of our larger practice peers to share knowledge.

Looking at journals, we can see completed projects that can claim low-carbon credentials and we can note the similarities of approach. However, without some form of benchmarking it's challenging to understand where our design processes, details and specifications are sitting within a wider spectrum of whole-life cycle energy use.

As architects we like the certainty that an iterative process can bring, so we adopted the simple but strategic tactic of implementing a whole-lifecycle assessment at [RIBA] Stage 2 and circularity assessment for each new project.

The choice of software was important, and we tested a range to decide the best fit for us. The modelling had to build confidence in its detail without absorbing large numbers of hours to input data. It had to deliver something visual for the client, with comparative metrics for the operational and embodied emissions, influencing various projected outcomes at the point in the design process where we can embed the key big wins of carbon reduction. FCBS CARBON was the right fit. By reviewing the initial embodied decisions with a similarly engaged small-practice M&E engineer, they were better placed to advise on the optimum design for operational energy. This may seem obvious, but smaller projects tend not to have an M&E engineer appointed at Stage 2. By creating a tangible uplift in the building's performance and quality, we are better placed to persuade future clients of the collaborative benefits.

It was heartening to see that our typical designs already performed well. We know local materials, are comfortable with forms of timber construction, and consider passive strategies before more expensive mechanical applications. We have done more retrofit than newbuild projects, which is possibly quite common for smaller practices, and this is a bank of knowledge that could be shared.

Where retrofit solutions aren't always feasible, we set an additional bar that all newbuild projects' whole lifecycle must significantly outperform a notional retrofit of the same size for carbon emissions, accessibility and circularity. The whole-life carbon assessment tool provides that platform to aim higher. The RIBA 2030 Challenge is certainly no barrier to the small practice and can be met with the right tools.

Next generation

By developing a tool that was designed to highlight the impact of design changes and so educate the user on how embodied carbon is emitted, we also produced a useful tool for universities and their students. Without the need for expensive software, and with a short learning curve, the students can explore their designs from a carbon perspective. This is a key step in reducing the built environment's environmental impact, encouraging the next generation of designers to engage and intuitively understand the impacts of their design decisions.

Rachel Harris, University of Sheffield

At the University of Sheffield School of Architecture, we decided to introduce FCBS CARBON to our third-year students within their final undergraduate environment and technology module.

I curated this module to combine subjects that will round off the students' education under the umbrella of whole-life carbon – allowing space to revisit subjects such as passive design principles in combination with introducing topics of embodied energy, retrofit and the circular economy.

The module sits directly alongside the design studio and requires an 'early-stage report', which asks the students to establish the environmental and technological aspirations of their design project. Within this we want students to experiment with a whole-life carbon review tool, particularly focusing on issues of embodied carbon, to add accountability and consequence realisation to their design decisions. FCBS CARBON is an easy-to-use tool that will enable quantifiable, comparative testing as opposed to previously relied-upon assumption and speculation.

Our students will shortly be entering practice and we envisage that the use of FCBS CARBON will help them to be at the forefront of this issue, alongside practices who are also just starting to grapple with issues of whole-life carbon and particularly embodied carbon.

It is hoped that using this tool as part of the wider course will teach our students to habitually consider whole-life carbon from a project outset. It will enable them to discuss environmental considerations not just in the abstract but give them the confidence as future architects to take ownership of projected project performance and metrics as an important part of their role as designers.

Conclusion

There is a lot of value in collaborative practice – in particular, to reach environmental goals and share knowledge. We are just one practice within a large industry, which in turn is part of a larger economic construct. FCBS CARBON is better because of the collaborative approach we took in the early stages of development and will have a bigger impact as a result.

There are plenty of other examples of collaboration taking place within the industry, with many breaching the old silos of knowledge and embracing cross-discipline working to achieve greater things. FCBStudios has embraced this approach by working with many groups, including:

- LETI
- Architects Declare
- Royal Institute of British Architects (RIBA)
- Chartered Institution of Building Services Engineers (CIBSE)
- Whole Life Carbon Network (WLCN)
- Architects Climate Action Netwwork (ACAN)
- UK Green Building Council (UKGBC)
- Part Z

These groups succeed through the generosity of their members giving their knowledge, time and enthusiasm, recognising that the climate crisis necessitates a new approach to sharing. But collaboration requires more than just sharing – it requires recognition of what we don't know, and working with those that do know the answers. The climate crisis will not be solved by hoarding knowledge, but by giving as much away as possible to those who need it.

1 Architects Declare, https://www.architectsdeclare.com/ (accessed 16 September 2022).
2 LETI, Embodied Carbon Primer, https://www.leti.uk/ecp (accessed 16 September 2022).
3 RICS, Whole Life Carbon Assessment for the Built Environment, November 2017, https://www.rics.org/globalassets/rics-website/media/news/whole-life-carbon-assessment-for-the–built-environment-november-2017.pdf (accessed 16 September 2022).

Community and Collaboration

An Experimental, Shared Approach to Working and Rising Together

WIP Collaborative: Abigail Coover, Bryony Roberts, Elsa Ponce, Lindsay Harkema, Ryan Brooke Thomas, Sera Ghadaki and Sonya Gimon

WIP (Work In Progress/Women In Practice) is an NYC-based community of women design professionals that cultivates shared knowledge and new collaborative models. WIP Collaborative is a shared practice of independent designers situated within this community. We assembled to work together on design and research projects, aiming to improve the public realm by foregrounding issues of equity, access and inclusivity. WIP Collaborative is democratically organised, and members contribute towards design and research endeavours in ways that suit our individual interests as well as the collective project goals.

Image of Restorative Ground by WIP Collaborative, a public streetscape installation in Lower Manhattan, 2021.

Collaboration is not fixed but is full of potential. It is inherently collective and participatory, and thrives on equity and adaptability. It can be an act of resistance, preventing decision-making and power from being concentrated in one person. Collaboration creates alternatives to existing hegemonic environments and systems. Through collaboration, we become individuals who rise together through co-creation.

WIP Collaborative is an experiment. As a flexible, shared practice within a network of women practitioners, it enables individuals to take on ambitious and inventive projects that would be less feasible for them to pursue on their own. As a work in progress, WIP aspires to foster a mutual reciprocity between the community and the collaborative, enabling a dynamic and continually evolving exchange of knowledge, experience and creative opportunity.

Lindsay Harkema: The idea for WIP developed through conversations with peer practitioners leading independent studios as well as those working in larger established firms. As individuals we were drawn to self-initiated practices, but also craved community connection. We desired professional support and resource-sharing as well as opportunities to work together. In conventional design practice, peer-to-peer competition is more pervasive than mutual support. WIP Community aims to foster a professional atmosphere in which we all rise together.

Women have historically been under-recognised and unsupported as leaders in architecture and design disciplines. In established offices, they are more often promoted as project managers, administrators and technical counterparts than as thought and design leaders. This could be a product of gender bias and patriarchal notions of the solo creative genius, perpetuated through the lineage of white male 'hero' architects that are disproportionately celebrated in the profession's history. It is also due to pervasive overwork and underpay that are incompatible with lifestyles that also include time for family and childcare responsibilities, emotional and bodily wellbeing, and civic-mindedness and activism. WIP aims to unlearn these negative characteristics and to learn from other values-driven collaborative groups to expand the narrative of shared labour.

Ryan Brooke Thomas: Collaboration presents an opportunity to work together in ways that support and promote our multiplicity as independent designers, thinkers and members of a community. For those of us who lead independent studios, pursuing a collective partnership is complementary to our individual practices in aspects of process, interaction, methodology and identity. The differences between the two are productive in stimulating individual creativity, nurturing career growth and opening us to new modes of working that draw from the diverse talents and perspectives of the group. WIP Collaborative's focus on projects that improve the public realm provides the opportunity to pursue an expanded set of project types with broader reach than is typically possible when working with private clients or commissions.

Collaboration can also yield productive surprises and lead to design outputs that are personal and characteristically different from what we would produce individually. We all share a common interest in working at the edges of our disciplines. In doing so, we aim to blur the boundaries between design expertise and expand the possibilities for practice. Experimental collaboration enables us to test ways of putting these values into action and to embrace the multifaceted nature of their implementation. The power implicit in collective dialogue can enable us to explore more radical positions (politically, socially, intellectually) and push ideas towards actionable efforts with priorities that can be broader in scope or more ambitious in impact than a traditional practice model.

Axonometric diagram of Restorative Ground, courtesy of WIP Collaborative.

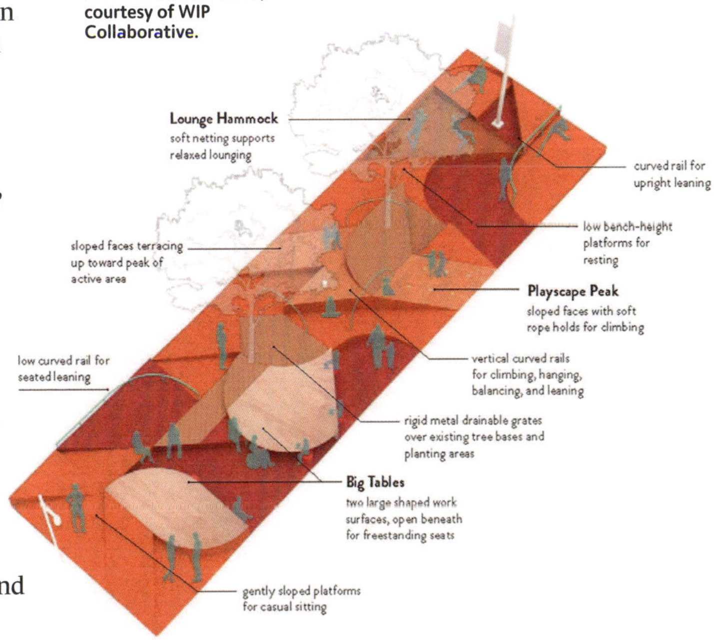

What have we learned from other collaborative practices, past and present?

Learning from other collaborative and co-creative groups is a form of research about how multiple identities and perspectives can come together, harnessing the power of their diversity, and achieving greater impact through collective action.

Bryony Roberts: The structure and methods of WIP Collaborative are inspired by contemporary and historical feminist practices. Like many of them, our goal is not just to advocate for gender equity, but to rethink the methods and goals of practice to address issues of equity more broadly in the built environment. We're interested in intersectional approaches to experiences of gender, sexuality, race, ability and class, and seek transformative methods of practice to address overlapping social inequities.

Examples of late 20th-century feminist practices in the UK are particularly inspiring to us. Groups such as Matrix Feminist Design Co-operative, Women's Design Service and muf architecture/art have developed innovative forms of non-hierarchical, cooperative and community-based practice that change both the internal power dynamics of the architecture office and the external relationships with communities. Matrix offered a model of a non-hierarchical office with a particularly expanded form of practice, which included client-based design work as well as research, community outreach, and the education of other women in construction and project management. Feminist Design Co-operative claimed a set of values focused on empowerment, participation and transparency through its collaborative endeavours. muf architecture/art offers meaningful examples of collaborative processes of co-creation with community partners. Practices like these have challenged the traditional power dynamics between architects and communities by valuing the lived experience of communities and the specialised expertise of architects.

Our feminist practice aims to bring attention to issues of embodiment in design. Historically, experiences of the body, of emotions and of pleasure have been gendered as female in the discipline of architecture. Feminist theorists like Donna Haraway and Maria Puig de la Bellacasa have emphasised the importance of embodied, lived experiences as a form of creative knowledge relative to constructed environments, both physical and political. Systemic conditions of social inequity shape everyday experiences of bodies and emotions. How can we as designers attend to both the scale of bodies and the scale of systems in ways of knowing and making? WIP foregrounds physicality and emotionality in public space, focusing on sensory experience and tactility, and partnering with self-advocates to conceive of spaces that can support a wider range of embodied experiences.

Related to embodiment, our design process is rooted in co-creation with communities in order to learn from their experiences. Expertise lives in the minds and bodies of individuals who navigate obstructive spaces and unsupportive environments in their everyday lives. By elevating their voices, we can engage self-advocates and designers in a shared vision for a better public realm.

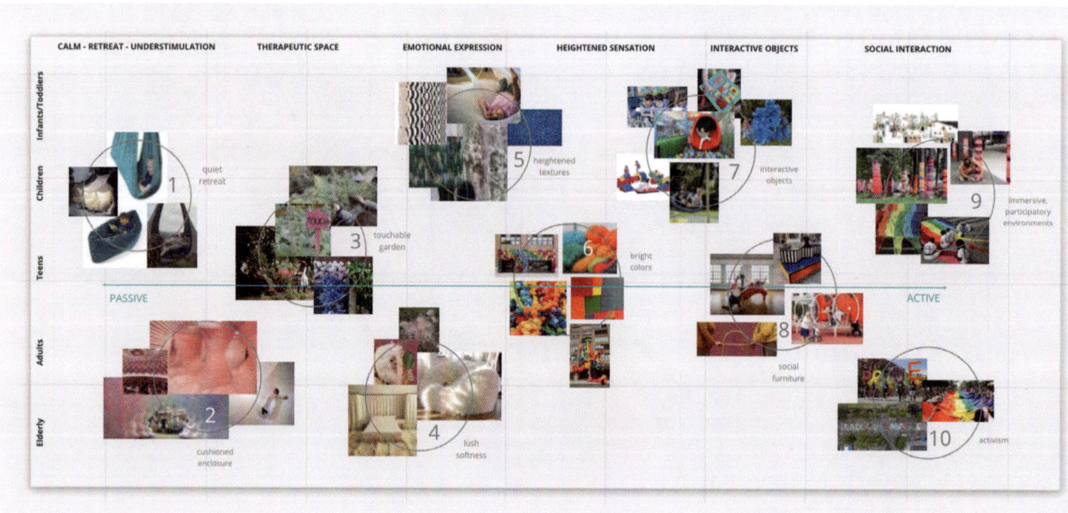

Image collage of spatial and textural references used for interviews with self-advocates in WIP's research about design for neurodiversity.

Aerial image of Restorative Ground, courtesy of Hudson Square Properties.

Ryan Brooke Thomas: In addition to feminist practices, we also draw inspiration from other creative collaboratives that pose alternative modes of organisation, process and output. We're interested in examples of non-hierarchical organisational structures that are inherently multifaceted and adaptive. Some contemporary examples include ConstructLab in Berlin, which is a collaborative practice that blends the design and construction processes to create built projects that are more responsive to their situated environments and the experiences of those participating in their creation. Here in NYC, the multidisciplinary design studio Urban Conga creates public activations through temporary installations and events that instigate opportunities for play in ways that are connected and responsive to local communities and groups of all ages. Studios like these offer alternatives to conventional built project timelines, positioning the process of creating and engaging with the work as equally if not more valuable than the final outcome.

We appreciate the values and codes of conduct of cooperative business structures that are owned and self-managed by their workers. Many of the core tenets of cooperatives align with our collective work ethos, such as shared leadership, supporting other values-driven organisations, prioritising labour ethics, and embracing democratic decision-making. We also draw inspiration and learn from our peers, mentors and other women in architecture, design, higher education and related disciplines. Our camaraderie and collaboration with other recently assembled collectives and activist groups, such as Design Advocates and Design as Protest, has bolstered our shared interest in questioning how the design of the built environment is conducted, and for whom.

Abigail Coover: We can learn from the successes and challenges of other collaboratives that prioritise underserved communities in the public realm. Such work is often ambitious and well received but restrained by a lack of funding or means of implementation. Having encountered similar challenges in our work, WIP pursues projects that direct funding and awareness towards these goals, as in as our research initiative with the Design Trust for Public Space and Verona Carpenter Architects. This work will entail a participatory analysis of existing public spaces with neurodiverse self-advocates and the

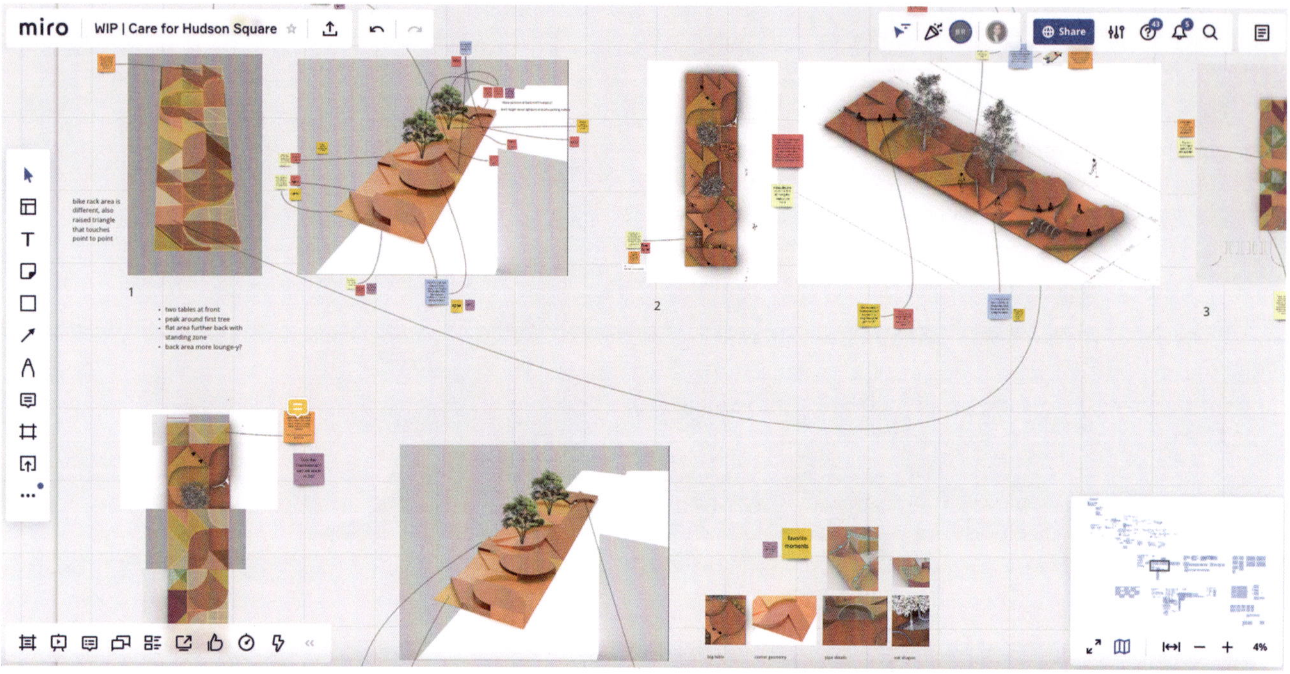

creation of design prototypes to inform policy reform for a more inclusive public realm.

The structure and organisation of WIP, including our aspirations and functional goals, is a project in itself. Many of our design peers are curious about our collective process. Who is the lead designer? How do we effectively design by committee? They are often surprised that our non-hierarchical structure applies to our process as well as our organisation. A common assumption is that design by committee can produce a compromised or inarticulate design. We find that working together as an egalitarian, multi-person team can elicit a more expansive approach that in the end strengthens the result. The process is not easier or more efficient than designing alone or with a small team, but the richness of the outcome is worth the effort of working collectively.

Our iterative design process utilises methods of co-creation, peer review, group design charrettes and an exquisite-corpse-like process of working through shared models, drawings and documents. In our collective work, efficiency is gained by working asynchronously with strategic opportunities for direct collaboration.

What have we unlearned from conventional design practice?

While the act of learning involves adding new skills or knowledge to an existing model, unlearning is the process of stepping outside an existing model in order to consciously create space for and pursue an alternative.

Elsa Ponce: The process of unlearning is a process of empowering alternatives to dominant structures and practices. The conventional identity of 'the architect' reflects current hegemonic systems that are authority based. As a society, we are used to systems of power (government, patriarchy, capitalism) that as individuals we cannot control. Many architecture practices adhere to similar hierarchies that reinforce the concentration of salary, authorship and decision-making power in the hands of a dominant few.

What is the alternative? A working environment in which individuals have a choice and decide what to contribute rather than just doing what they are told; a collective structure that is more just and equitable. WIP Collaborative enables us to act wilfully and unlearn behaviours of dominance. To make space to build new skills and reciprocities as well as to learn and practise self-awareness within a collective framework. By unlearning the notion that we have to change our individual selves to perform better, we can combine strengths, desires and methodologies to improve the way we perform together.

Traditional design practices rely on a competitive culture that pits individuals against rather than in support of each other. Designers learn to constantly compare their performance and accomplishments against their peers', cultivating an atmosphere of fear and anxiety that can negatively impact an individual's mental health and wellbeing. How can we avoid these toxic conditions in our collaboration? It begins by accepting and celebrating the fact that no project is realised by a single author and by better understanding the people that you work with and depend on.

Sera Ghadaki: The circumstances of the pandemic have pushed us towards alternative structures of thinking and doing in the past two years. Social isolation caused by quarantine, protests against racial inequities embedded in our society, and heightened anxiety and trauma surrounding loss have disrupted our previous ways of life. Moving forward requires unlearning on various levels, including unlearning the patterns of the now defunct 'normal' that allowed systemic injustice to persist, and responding to the impacts of our collective anxiety and trauma. Unlearning is part of adapting to change, whether on a global, community or individual scale.

Opposite: Screenshot of a digital whiteboard used in WIP's collaborative design process.

Below: Image of Restorative Ground courtesy of WIP Collaborative.

Above: Diagram of experiential zones in Restorative Ground, courtesy of WIP Collaborative.

Below: Post-occupancy analysis drawing of Restorative Ground, courtesy of WIP Collaborative.

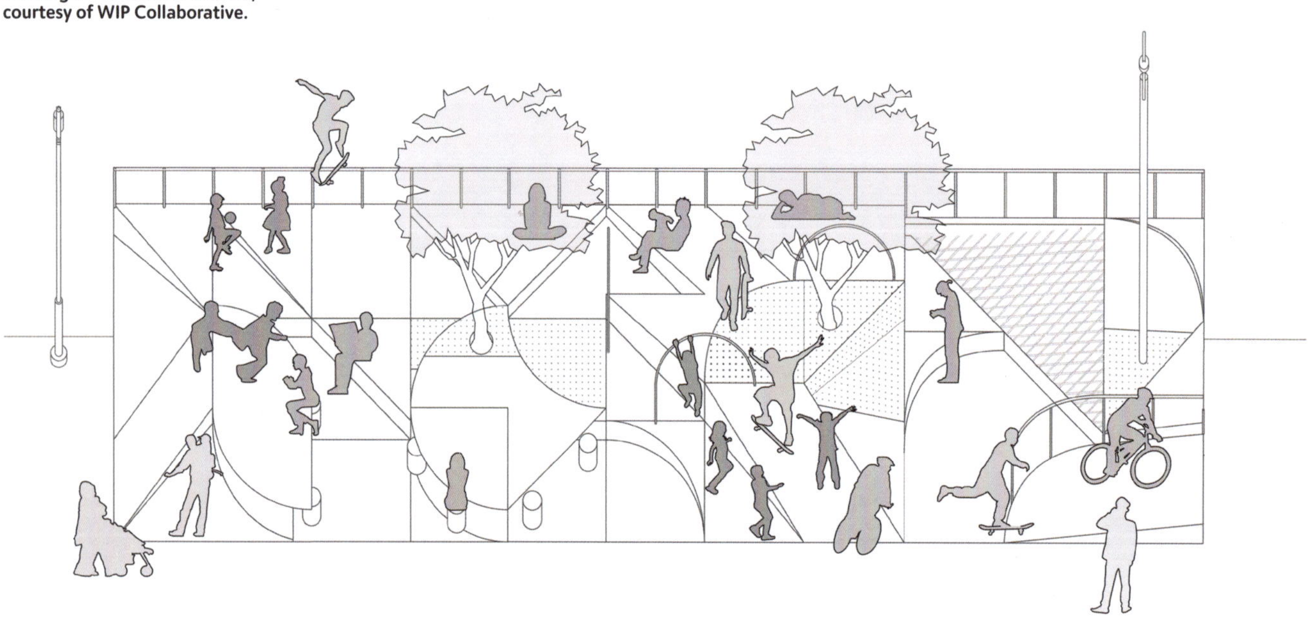

How have our projects tested and shaped our approach to collaboration? What challenges or opportunities for improvement have we encountered?

WIP's range of projects includes self-initiated research, commissioned temporary public installations, public realm design consulting for urban architecture projects of different scales, and multiphased public space analysis, prototyping and policymaking initiatives in collaboration with other designers, nonprofit organisations and community partners. Though all projects are approached collectively, the dedicated team of designers can grow or shrink as needed. For longer-term projects, individuals might be more involved during different phases, allowing each of us to step forward and back according to interest, relevant expertise and personal schedule.

Our first built project was a public streetscape installation in Lower Manhattan entitled 'Restorative Ground' that was completed in July 2021. The installation offers a landscape of choice – different zones of experiential conditions, geometry, material textures and spatial qualities. As a public streetscape, the project required coordination with multiple city agencies for necessary permitting and approvals. Our combined skillset proved effective to meet the range of knowledge and experience needed and maintain collective involvement throughout the project.

Sera Ghadaki: Throughout the phases of creating Restorative Ground, we self-organised based on individual interest, experience and availability in response to project demands. Appointed teams managed correspondence with external entities and provided updates in order for everyone to stay informed about the status of work. Communicating through Slack channels, shared Google documents and regular Zoom meetings, we learned to optimise our workflow by balancing asynchronous work and focused collaboration. Complementing this primarily remote collaboration were key moments of gathering in smaller teams for fabrication reviews, site visits or material selection hand-offs.

After completion, we conducted a study to learn about how the project is used by the public. We invited the fresh perspective of a new team member to conduct this effort to better understand the performative characteristics of the installation. This was an opportunity to explore methods for collecting both quantitative and qualitative data, documenting intangible characteristics such as sensorial experiences and emotionality, and surveying users engaging with the installation through observation, conversation and questioning.

Ryan Brooke Thomas: Restorative Ground enabled us not only to test a collaborative approach to the project brief but also to see the potential of combining our different skillsets. The team's experience spans a range of professional roles, design disciplines and project types. The framework of the project and our process provided an opportunity for each of us to shift gears and to wear different hats throughout its timeline. We experienced how this way of working could activate a dynamic feedback loop of exchanged ideas and collective contribution as well as identify learning opportunities for future improvement. Ultimately, the process reinforced our interest in exploring the possibilities for collective practice, fostering a platform for experimentation, and expanding beyond traditional formats for design production and agency.

Time is a finite resource, but energy is expandable. In addition to broadening an individual's capacity, our adaptive framework offers the opportunity to renew and augment our energy through a shared ethos. We try to replace energy-depleting habits such as putting in long hours and working without a sense of purpose with energy-fuelling practices like establishing shared meaning and contributing with what each of us is best at and enjoys doing. Each of us has her own rituals for energy renewal – taking breaks, focusing at certain times of the day, and maintaining awareness of her susceptibility to negative emotions. We strive to enrich rather than deplete each other by acknowledging these different needs and by fostering an environment where we feel inspired, engaged and fulfilled.

Screenshot from a Zoom meeting with WIP Collaborative founding members.

WIP Organisational Diagram (work in progress), courtesy of WIP Collaborative.

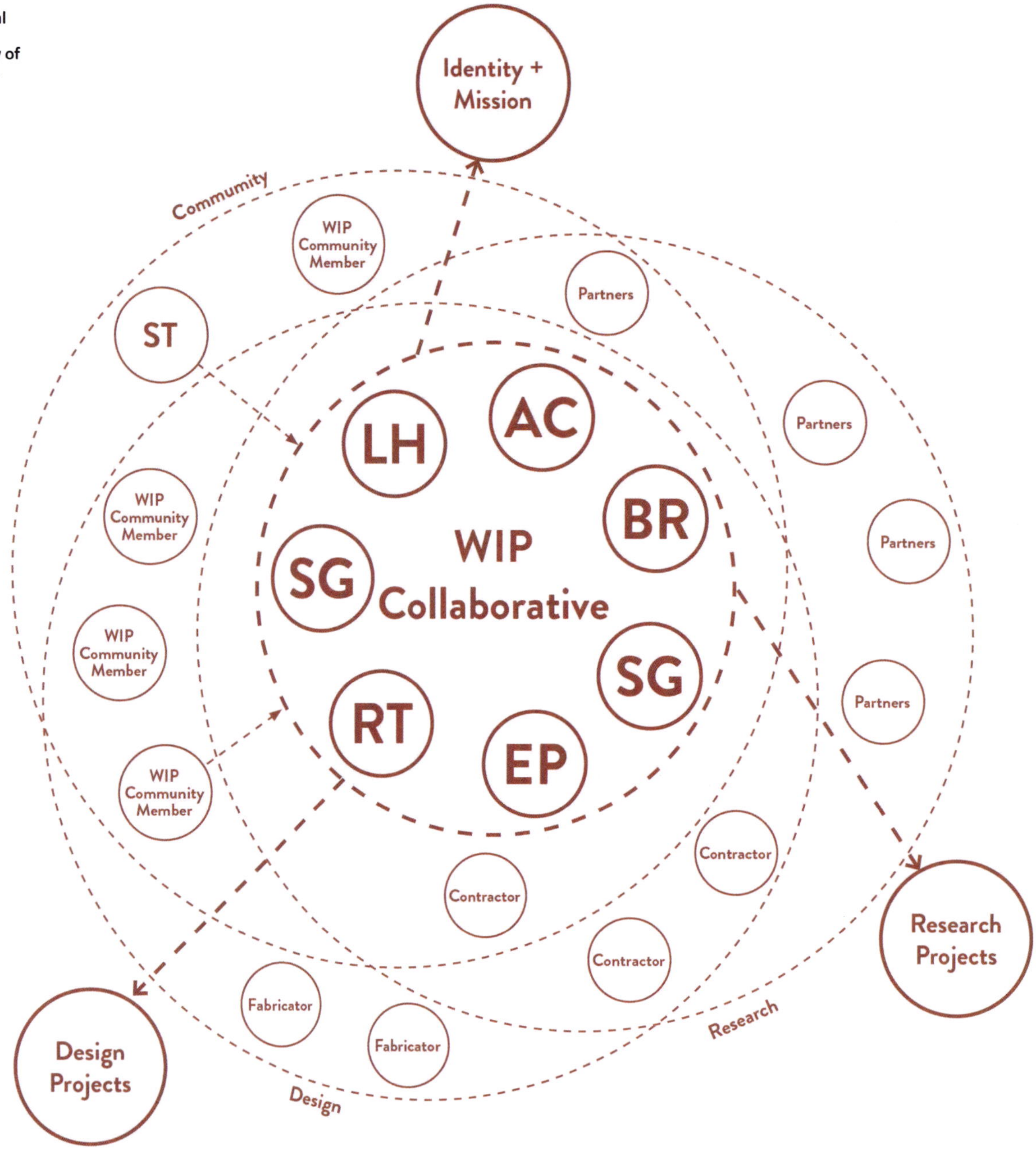

How might WIP evolve in the future?

One challenge of experimental practice is longevity – how will a new model become sustainable over time? As a society we are grappling with the reality that static and inflexible structures are unequipped to effectively respond and adapt to necessary changes. The open-endedness of WIP is an investment in its future evolution. This is a shared trait with other recently formed collaborative groups. Having assembled at a time of immense upheaval in so many aspects of collective life, it makes sense that our organisations are inherently indeterminate. The uncertain circumstances of the present have also enabled us to continually improvise and make the most of what we have by pooling resources, working strategically, and leaning on each other in order to be effective.

Sonya Gimon: How does the flexibility of a collaborative coexist with the value of having an established, tight-knit team? An individual might contribute differently to different projects at different times, making space for others to become more involved. Valuing an individual's unique contribution while acknowledging the need for a cohesive approach is inherent to our collaboration.

Driven by interest in exploring pressing topics through both research and design, we see including the perspectives of experts and self-advocates as an invaluable part of our work. Through interviews, workshops and other forms of community engagement, we aim to incorporate a wider range of experience and creative potential into design insights and tangible solutions.

Lindsay Harkema: One exciting aspect of WIP Collaborative is its potential for future transformation. Though we have operated primarily as the team of seven founding members, we believe team diversity and flexibility is necessary for different projects. More recently the WIP Collaborative team has included other members like Sasha Topolnytska, an architectural and product designer who joined our design for neurodiversity research team.

By combining strengths and interests, we can tackle unconventional project types – innovative public installations, speculative research, public-realm-focused design consulting, and holistic pre-design planning combining ecological, social and architectural design goals. Building on this experience, we're working to craft a clearer narrative of how this adaptive model of collaborative practice is beneficial to projects and clients, and how it sets us apart from conventionally organised firms.

By operating outside of disciplinary norms, WIP Collaborative is capable of projects that are inherently open-ended and undefined at the outset. We've been asked to propose ideas for exterior and interior spaces that lack a determined use or intent – they might be temporarily vacant, or adjacent to more specifically programmed spaces, or intersect with the public realm but are underutilised and lack purpose. Our commitment to community engagement, alternative design modes and materialities, social equity and shared embodiment enable us to take a holistic, multifaceted and optimistic design approach to open-ended opportunities. These are the projects we aim for – endeavours in which there is a reciprocity between how we work as a collaborative team and how the work develops in different and expansive ways.

WIP emerged from the shared sentiments and interests of a peer group seeking new modes of collaboration and professional support. We hope its adaptable framework can serve as a prompt for others pursuing alternative forms of creative practice, by offering experimental methods for designing and working together. Key to all of this is an openness to change, mutual trust and a commitment to inclusive empowerment by and for everyone involved.

In-Sourcing

Experiments in Organising a 21st-Century Architecture Studio

Khuzema Hussain, Siri Zanelli, Alasdair Ben Dixon and Tomas Tvarijonas, Collective Works

Above: A small project with a larger purpose: the Outdoor Classroom at Highgate Primary School. We make room for a variety of projects for a variety of clients; this imaginary world of plywood and colour was co-designed with the children.

Right: We try constantly to question and challenge how we run our business, so we can enjoy work and improve ourselves simultaneously. From left: Tomas, Alasdair, Siri, Jade, Joe and Khuzema, celebrating 10 years of Collective Works, and still smiling.

There are many reasons to challenge the status quo in architecture. We know that the projects we work on shape the lives of our clients as well as those who visit, pass by or in any way experience the buildings we create. Simultaneously, we know that there is no such thing as a separation between 'work' and 'life'; the relationships we form as professionals can be as meaningful and important as those we grew up with.

Our work can be enormously positive both for people's lives and planetary health if carefully crafted with consideration for the other. It can also cause unintended harms when environmental and social impact go unconsidered. Within the profession there has been a reckoning regarding the often-problematic nature of our workplaces, where long hours, unpaid work and discrimination persist.

We're exploring our agency in relation to these issues and see collaboration as key to their resolution. We encourage anyone reading this to consider their role in shaping a better world and to reflect on this call to action from Alan Moore – who, along with many others, is inspiring us to do better:

You are a builder of a new way of living and working, creating a new business for a new age, with a new vision.

Alan Moore, *Do Build: How to Make and Lead a Business the World Needs*[1]

Playful co-creation

Collective Works is not a static studio with rigid rules, but a project in its own regard. We are experimenting with what it takes to build a responsible and beautiful business capable of creating responsible and beautiful design.

Early in our journey, we understood that running an ethical business would be a process of iteration, of trial and error, and would require a commitment to working differently and pushing things forward. Everyone is shaped by their experiences. We realised that what was the canon within the architecture industry 10 years ago is no longer fit for the 21st century. And we can accept that what is appropriate now will need to adapt to be fit for purpose in another 10 years' time.

We want to help create the world in which we would like to live, with regard to architecture but also business. To do that, we want everyone within Collective Works to see their work as part of a larger purpose. This creates space for a sense of identity, purpose and self-worth. And it allows the studio itself to take on a process of reinvention in order to create more impact.

Working collectively: now and the future, what went right

Flexibility benefits all

There is a way of finding a win for the company and a win for the individual. Part-time contracts are our approach. With more team members working part-time, we can bring more minds on to each project. And for our team, this creates the opportunity to work in parallel with studies; to pursue other interests or roles; to simply have liberty in their week. This arrangement is discussed at biannual reviews, and so far no one has preferred a full-time permanent contract. Most of our team have been with us for many years, and we are as protective of their contracts as we would be if they were employees.

Twinned with time flexibility came location flexibility. Why require people to work in front of us? Not only are we regularly away from our desks, but also if we allow people the time to fit other things into their week, then inevitably, they may wish to work in a place more optimal to their commute. We recognised another truism about finding balance: much of architectural work is concentrated tasks while the design process necessarily injects shots of creative disruption. And that is our target: to have at least one day a week in a shared space where creativity is unleashed, while the remainder of the week is reserved for more concentrated work, wherever a person is most comfortable and effective.

In June 2019, we gave a talk at the RIBA on why flexible work was not just possible, but essential in architecture.[2] So when the sweeping impact of Covid-19 came along, we were not at all panicked about how to carry on collaborating. And now in the post-lockdown context, we're still holding on to the belief that flexibility will continue to offer advantages.

We try to strike a balance between flexible working and an inclusive, creative workplace with a culture of togetherness. This is Khuzema and Jade in the studio, where Wednesdays are for working together.

The power of diversity

The human brain is impressive, but the success of the human species consists in the intricate web of connections, stretching across the planet and back through history, which has led to a vast body of ideas, technologies, and culture. For an estimated two million years this has guided the process of human genetic evolution, expanding the brain, altering our physiology, and feeding back into the body of ideas, technologies, and culture. Our species is, in this sense, constructed upon diversity.

Matthew Syed, *Rebel Ideas: The Power of Diverse Thinking*[3]

Our collective mind is much more powerful than any individual genius. Even as a small office, we're structured in a way to think bigger. The partners themselves sit at very different places on the personality spectrum, which an early coach remarked upon and we ensured would be beneficial when we leveraged our varied perspectives. Thankfully, creating architecture and running a business require a combination of the strategic, the social and the technical.

We recognise that broadening our diversity further will mean increased innovation and creativity,[4] as homogeneity is reduced, and more holistic decisions are taken with fewer inherent biases.

Our team currently comprises 25% global majority, which is above the UK average but lower than the London average, which was around 40% in the 2019 census.[5] A large proportion of our work is in London, and 75% of our team are based here.

The Design Council recently underwent substantive change from its own research about unconscious bias within the design process; we would concur that the more closely our team reflects the society we wish to serve, the greater the sensitivity of our work to one of the most diverse cities on the planet. We've also calculated both our gender and ethnicity pay gaps, which while easily skewed in a small business still have some way to go.

Inclusion is not about bringing people into what already exists; it is about creating a new space, a better space for everyone.

George J Sefa Dei, 'Rethinking the role of indigenous knowledges in the academy'[6]

Beyond meeting targets, we recognise that diversity isn't enough and that we must embrace inclusion as well as continuing to use our voices to call for change in our stubbornly unrepresentative industry.

Above: When the pandemic took hold in 2020, we were already used to working remotely and collaborating online, so the largest change was for those of us with children who suddenly had to share the home office.

Below: Fundraiser and public consultation at Omved Gardens for an artist workshop.

Hierarchy and collaboration

The path to collaboration begins with putting egos aside. Leaders in business of course have experience which younger members of the team do not; however, good ideas can come from anywhere. Younger staff are often better aligned with the changing world and offer valuable perspectives on the tried-and-tested – and possibly tired – wisdom of the past.

Our common mission is great projects, and in architecture the constraints are manifold. Collaboration creates richness and even efficiency – but requires an invitation to others to not only contribute but also to be heard. There is of course a distinction between a cacophony and a chorus, and we would argue that it takes a leadership that listens. Allowing individuals the space for accountability and agency creates a better team that can focus its collective energy on a project.

Working collectively: the first few years – what didn't go so right

If we all learn more from our mistakes than our successes, surely it is in the interest of pedagogy and the betterment of the profession to share our trials and tribulations? Rarely does Plan A succeed – but it is rather the lessons learned through experiments that lead to a plan that does.

Building the right team

We started our journey into collaboration by learning from the software industry and creating a network of interesting people who could adroitly and expertly assist projects. This is a prime example of where theory meets practice and how even good ideas – particularly from afield – need translation.

Our earliest work was competition submissions and self-driven projects. These gave us a false confidence that we were on to a winning organisational model. Colleagues with masterplan experience joined us to create a plan for a new tramline and townscape in Greece, graphic designers helped us create branding and collateral, and we had many minds join the brainstorm for our temporary theatre. But for domestic renovation – the basis for a lot of income in a small studio – there was no real need, and certainly no real fee, for additional specialists. It turned out that trying to cross-pollinate infrastructure work and rear extensions belonged more to the island of Doctor Moreau than London. There was simply no real need for a unique team of free agents for bread-and-butter work.

An additional challenge – and one that beleaguers us to this day – is resourcing. Keeping tabs on who is doing what is hard enough. And while software tools help in the management process, for a start-up architecture studio, we had neither the nous nor cash to have one of these in place. So we were forever chasing our dream team about their availability, their deliverables and their invoices (because we insisted on paying everyone, even if it was for an hour's work).

The right people that create a great team are essential to any organisation. Our lesson learned: it's hard enough to find those people and create a team; organisational innovation is a safer bet than organisational revolution.

Experiments in communal working

In our excitement to do and be the future of architectural practice – certainly with regard to organisation – we pushed boundaries everywhere we could. That in and of itself was a mistake, as we didn't pick our battles wisely but rather empirically. One of our experiments was to position ourselves amid the public. After a kind invitation from a friend and studio neighbour, Mark, we set up shop within The Common E2, a coffee place in Bethnal Green. We wanted to explore the boundaries between architect and client, and so we rented a bank of tables along one side of the cafe.

We learned the power of community as the coffee shop became a new hub for the various businesses adjacent to the premises. But we also learned the value of peace and quiet. We had inadvertently traded this in for our proximity to potential punters. And the trade-off of espresso machine music in exchange for job

The Common E2 – our first workspace was in a coffee shop. We have matured into our own studio space, but remain flexible.

opportunities just did not materialise. Both concentrated work and privacy remain as challenges for us even now that we have our own small studio; phone calls, Zoom meetings and even management conversations can distract those around.

Understanding our audience

In 2016 we took to the stage at the Archiboo Architect Pitch,[7] an opportunity for seven studios to present an elevator pitch to a panel of built-environment veterans. The winner is promised a relationship with a developer, so the event makes good business sense.

We resolutely advocated collaboration and a network of like-minded individuals to coalesce into a team that would be far greater than the sum of its parts. This was of course – and is still, though to a lesser extent – far from the traditional model of practice. Our pitch was met with confusion and some ridicule. The experience was somewhat traumatic at the time, as we not only confidently believed in the idea but also were successfully delivering projects this way. As collectives are now in vogue, we were clearly early adopters of an idea that had in fact excited the audience of architects but less so the panel of potential clients.

And this was our great lesson: to speak to the person – or group – in front of you. We have separate marketing material for homeowners, for developers and for community-based organisations; basically, something specific for every audience. Although obvious now, it took us some time to put ourselves in the shoes of the people thinking of appointing us.

Rob reflecting on our infamous Archiboo pitch at our tenth birthday party. Alasdair had spoken of flexible, remote working, and collaborative teams, long before the industry was interested.

The internal workings of a collaborative practice

Contracts

We've been promoting flexibility in architectural practice since our inception in 2012. We try to go beyond 'discouraging' long hours and have found a way that works in our practice to empower our team to keep projects – and their own time – within agreed hours.

Our team all work as contractors, on fixed-term contracts usually 6 to 12 months long. They all have part-time contracts, which allow them the flexibility to pursue education and other interests/work, or simply spend time with family. They can also then do their work when it suits them, not only from where it suits them. We find this works well, and of course, trust goes both ways: we trust them to complete their tasks and they trust us to manage their workload and keep them engaged.

Pay

One of the most maligned aspects of using contractors is the general view that companies leverage their position to minimise pay. And following from this attitude is the concept that surely companies shouldn't trust contractors to be loyal and value-aligned members of the team. We have been willing to contend with those views and to share our experience of a different way forward.

From our outset, we tested several remuneration models. We had a commission scheme for co-workers who brought us jobs. And we paid hourly for specialist co-workers to attend charrettes and produce distinct deliverables. We even trialled a form of universal basic income, rewarding all those within our network for simply contributing to our culture. Outwardly we set up joint ventures with other studios – small and large – to better undertake projects that lay slightly outside our comfort zone.

And by now, we have a much better idea of what works for us. At Collective Works, we set our pay rates in line with RIBA's annual benchmark. And with the help of our accountant, we ensure that leave benefits, pension allocations and even IT costs are compared, so team remuneration is equivalent to that of an employee. We also addressed the cost-of-living crisis with one-off supplement payments starting early summer 2022, and make sure we have social days, lunches and outings covered as benefits. Given the efficiency with which our team operates, it gives us some satisfaction to know that in most cases we can end up paying above the median.

Cooperative career development

It is a misunderstanding to align opportunities for career growth with the size of a studio, especially one based on

Above: Being female and majority led was not a strategic choice but remains a strength. We want to continue to build a team of people who are not too similar, to ensure we don't design within an echo chamber.

Below: Striking the balance between creative work and collaboration, and efficient concentrated thinking and production, is still a work in progress. We choose to have a studio space to ensure we can come together in person to share ideas and enjoy each other's company.

networks. As with most things, intention comes first and then ways can be found. We of course leverage our small studio environment to allow management conversations to be overheard and for individuals to assist on any number of business needs. However, we also make sure that no one is forever doing the same kind of drawing, at the same stage of work or on the same type of project.

Recently we have set up new internal aims to take us to the next decade. And one of them is to create a culture of learning. We've allocated at least 10% of everyone's time to R&D and knowledge-sharing. We want our co-workers to feel as if they share the values of the company. And as part of this team, they can then individually pursue learning interests which are not only good for their careers but also align to our collective ambitions.

Hybrid working

At Collective Works, we wanted to avoid issues of presenteeism, a longstanding problem in our industry. We also wanted to acknowledge that day-to-day challenges can come just as much from childcare as caring for elderly parents. And while care responsibilities have traditionally kept women out of the workforce, we recognise that many men would also like to spend more time with their loved ones.

Although flexible working has long been the norm at Collective Works, post-lockdown, we along with the rest of the working world are at an inflection point where hybrid working needs better definition. One of our recent shifts has been to create a calendar of togetherness that will find balance between the physical and virtual. We try to manage calendars so that Wednesday is the studio day where the majority attend for design sessions, ad hoc discussions and some socialising. Alongside this are more formalised project reviews, which can be undertaken remotely but still allow the team to come together and focus their attention.

Contractors and overtime

Previously we demonstrated that having contractors had mutual advantages. One such positive relates to resourcing and overtime. Contractors are officially contracted to tasks/scope; however, in practice, their agreements are linked to time. With terms usually based on hourly rates, asking contractors to exceed their scope quickly runs up the tab. And so, efficient work and good time management suddenly become necessary. Which in turn avoids unexpected overtime.

As a starting point, the partners are vigilant about monitoring changes of scope; many time pressures are alleviated by identifying requests to do something other than what was agreed. And with the help of project architects, we have weekly progress updates to make sure that projects run within their allocated time budgets. And with the right empowerment, our co-workers are now comfortable pushing back on partners' requests for more design such that overworking a project is done rarely, and then only with full awareness. Managing deadlines is often as simple as respecting everyone's time and prioritising correctly.

Turning our backs on the overtime culture has been healthy for the business, as it puts us in a position where we must manage the time spent on projects rigorously. We are better equipped to upsell our services and encourage clients to consider the way their input and communication styles guide the projects.

Considered communication

Asynchronous communication is key to remote work. It means that information is not required to be read right away. Instead, it can be produced when convenient for one person and read when convenient for another.

Unlike meetings, calls and WhatsApp messages that require immediate attention, asynchronous methods allow you to work on tasks when you decide to. Your focus is no longer bombarded with notifications and urgent calls to action, providing a respite for mental health. Over time, the knowledge collected in these depositories can be systemised into templates, guides and other systems storing the collective knowhow. Every concept design report template, colour palette and onboarding routine should have the mistakes and successes of past experiences embedded. This way, the knowledge is distributed to everyone in the team, and the workflow no longer relies on a few select individuals being involved.

Asynchronous communication does not work for everything. Direct connection is still critical for creativity, lateral thinking and collaboration. Empathy can also get lost in between lines of text. So scheduling times for people to get together is essential. Pick the right tool for the job. The goal is not to never see your co-workers again. Instead, it is to recognise that everyone has different working habits, and to utilise this difference to make the business more profitable, humane and successful.

Ruthless balance

There needs to be a ruthlessness to the management of an architectural studio for us to adhere to our values. The business is an ecosystem and must be finely balanced for design to thrive, individuals to live and the company to survive.

Our goal is to strengthen the culture of focused work and calendar planning such that we can follow in others' footsteps of having a four-day week. A well-rested, healthy and mentally refreshed team is much more likely to come up with good ideas and take projects to higher standards, and of course, enjoy working together.

A need for flexibility was the catalyst for Collective Works. And ten years later, it has evolved into a pursuit for work–life integrity.

> *When someone has work-life integrity, it means that they feel empowered in all areas of their life and that they are able to give the time and attention they desire to each of those areas.*
>
> Global Wellness Institute, 'Workplace wellbeing: Initiative resources'[8]

We'll continue to pursue responsibility and beauty in our work and where necessary question our industry, to call for more robust discourse on the challenges we all face. We hope that by exploring some new pathways in practice and sharing our experiences we can spare others from making our mistakes and encourage them to take some new risks for the good of others on this journey.

Moving away from the screens is part of building company culture: company trip to Norway.

1 Alan Moore, *Do Build: How to Make and Lead a Business the World Needs*, The Do Book Co., 2021.
2 RIBA, 'Pushing boundaries: LFA small talks', https://www.architecture.com/whats-on/pushing-boundaries-lfa-small-talks (accessed 20 September 2022).
3 Matthew Syed, *Rebel Ideas: The Power of Diverse Thinking*, John Murray, 2019.
4 McKinsey & Company, 'Diversity wins: How inclusion matters', May 2020, https://www.mckinsey.com/~/media/mckinsey/featured%20insights/diversity%20and%20inclusion/diversity%20wins%20how%20inclusion%20matters/diversity-wins-how-inclusion-matters-vf.pdf (accessed 20 September 2022).
5 Office for National Statistics, 'Population estimates by ethnic group and religion, England and Wales: 2019', https://www.ons.gov.uk/peoplepopulationandcommunity/populationandmigration/populationestimates/articles/populationestimatesbyethnicgroupandreligionenglandandwales/2019 (accessed 26 September 2022).
6 George J Sefa Dei, 'Rethinking the role of indigenous knowledges in the academy', International Journal of Inclusive Education, 10 November 2010, https://doi.org/10.1080/13603110028484 9.
7 Caro, 'The return of the architect pitch', https://carocommunications.com/archiboo-the-architect-pitch/ (accessed 20 September 2022).
8 Global Wellness Institute, 'Workplace wellbeing: Initiative resources', https://globalwellnessinstitute.org/initiatives/workplace-wellbeing-initiative/workplace-wellbeing-initiative-resources/ (accessed 20 September 2022).

Building a Dream Team

Scales of Collaboration

Marc Cairns and Samuel Stair, New Practice

Visualisation of the worthwhile use for the Cambridge Core Site.

What constitutes a team on an architectural project? Where do its confines and scope end? Does the 'team' constitute the direct design team itself, or the wider consultants and contractors involved?

Marc Cairns, Managing Director, New Practice

On its journey to completion, the boundaries of a project's respective teams overlap or are redrawn as its shifts in responsibility and (unexpected) variables reveal themselves over time. With this understanding, teamwork doesn't hinge upon responsibility or the realm of liability, and isn't a top-down network of discrete members; rather, its foundation is the shifting exchange between relationships in collaboration.

The notion of fluid and adaptable partnership is fundamental in any 'dream team', and a core principle in the work and workings of New Practice. Collaboration is intuitive at New Practice, with its very beginnings founded on the academic collaboration between our directors Marc Cairns and Becca Thomas. When establishing a practice from nothing, with nothing, with no Bank of Mum and Dad and no clients, one has to find ways to draw on teamwork with others to build, grow, learn and ultimately make and do what you love. There has been a continual necessity to call upon our 'intuitive collaboration' as projects and circumstances present ever-changing challenges or opportunities. In this, there is a need to recognise what you're good at and what you're not, to relinquish the ego of the architect, and to know when an artist, writer, designer or engineer knows more than you; understanding these complex factors of accountability, knowledge and process, and working within, rather than alongside or against, them yields more genuine and richer outcomes which respond to and resonate with a wider audience.

Beyond a working process, collaboration is also itself a business model for New Practice. As a small practice of 10 people it allows us to work on some of the most important built environment projects across the UK, delivering creative and best-practice, place-based design and community engagement. This in turn raises the profile of New Practice across the industry through our treasured, fostered relationships, while resulting in work which draws attention through the very processes of partnership itself.

For collaboration to provide the above results, it must be authentic and offer genuine mutual benefit; good teamwork is interactive, not extractive. Further, it must be based on kindness – we often find ourselves the 'junior party' on projects, and the experience of this can be positive or negative; it gives us a responsibility to not replicate the negative experiences, but to work through them and provide a duty of care for many of those we collaborate with.

To forge and foster the above form of collaboration, three things must be actioned:

1. *Relinquishing ego* – a collaboration is inherently a meeting of parties in an attempt to work together, which requires mutual respect. Even in working scenarios where a hierarchy (of experience, scope or contract, for instance) is in place, for collaboration to be fruitful it must be approached as a group of equals, and flow horizontally rather than vertically.
2. *Listening* – collaborations of this nature are intra-relations, not inter-relations, for the parties collaborating must always be working in an interconnected manner where they evolve together, rather than as two discrete entities. For this to occur, there must be a consistent and active attempt from each party to listen to all others.
3. *Confidence* – with the previous two points actioned, what remains is the confidence to be a contributing member of the collaboration. Speak up, and ensure that your voice is heard within it so that the collaboration doesn't stall and become unbalanced; however, always in tandem with an effort to enact the first two points in turn.

The above guides produce collaborations that foster confidence, allowing others to be seen through ego and actively heard; it is often such collaborations that yield the most unique, inventive and fruitful outcomes, which would otherwise likely go undiscovered. However, there is no defined form of these collaborations – they change, evolve and respond to the relational environment within which they are born. Yet, there are trends, common scales and methods that develop over time, and allow you to understand your own 'morphology of collaboration'.

As in the iterative design of a project, collaborations occur at different scales – but this similarity doesn't end at size or scope. In design, each scale has a distinct benefit and use, a time and application where it is deemed either useful or impractical. The same is true for collaboration, its different modes called upon in a project when practical and required. A good designer wouldn't design a flashing detail at 1:10,000, nor a site plan at 1:5. In the same way, different tasks require different scales of partnership for maximum efficacy. It's not just about detail, it's also about learning, revealing and imparting knowledge. It's

Live illustrations of pop-up engagement for the Newham Characterisation Study.

about the degree of intimacy versus comprehensiveness with the content. As in successful and seemingly effortless design, virtuosity in teamwork comes with the mixing or crossing of scales. For instance, while it's not practical to design a site plan at 1:5, incorporating a degree of that intimacy into a different perspective can uncover or spark something that would have gone unnoticed before. Following are six examples of the 'scale of collaboration' called upon at New Practice, drawing from projects we've been actively working on between 2021 and 2022.

Scales of collaboration

1:1 / Intimate: Detail – Newham Characterisation Study

Sadie's work is beautiful and characterful. Commissioning local creatives, experts and organisations, like her, is often the best route to a more meaningful relationship with the community.

Duncan Bain, Associate, New Practice

With the most potent degree of learning, when used in design the 'largest' scale is represented in equal proportion to the subject; this fosters a mutual relationship between the two in which development and uncovering in the design process is an act of to-and-fro. Working at this scale reveals a deeper understanding of the work at hand, and this is also the case when collaborating at a 1:1 human scale.

During our work in east London for the Newham Characterisation Study, we realised early in the process that it was important to engage a local voice to assist in forming our approach and communication, and tailoring activities for the success of the project. Hence, upon the advice of a local artist, already a contact of ours, we began a collaboration with illustrator Sadie St. Hilaire. With Sadie forming part of the team on the project, we were able to learn in richer detail from someone immersed in the cultural and urban grain of the area, and attuned to its identity, perspectives and voices. This reflects the mutualistic exchange of imparting and learning characteristic to this scale of collaboration, which beyond an extractive act of engagement, saw Sadie's input reveal new directions for the project itself. The task of producing illustrations that resonated with the local community grew into the production of risograph material at Rabbits Road Press (an independent printing press local to the area), combined with Sadie's continued engagement in producing live illustrations of our team members consulting the public on the ground in Newham. Sadie's detailed perspective encouraged a mutual back and forth, deciding together, and the nudging of our approach into an increasingly perfect fit. The outcome of this allowed us to communicate with the people of Newham in a nuanced manner that was 'inherently Newham', articulating the questions and progress of the consultation by reflecting the figures, activities and faces recognisable by the population, moving them from being a 'target community' to 'front and centre' in the project's journey.

1:10 / Expert: Exchange – High Street Heritage

As a heritage professional I have long advocated the potential multiple benefits of transdisciplinary working. Working on this project with the wonderful team at New Practice has proved me right.

Dr Alan Leslie, Heritage Specialist

A step outward from 1:1 brings us to a scale that presents detailed elements as a whole, in which they can be understood and read in conjunction with other similarly scaled elements to form a readable group with wider focus. The same is true in collaboration with experts, where individual discursive elements are presented in their entirety, through the perspective of a complete knowledge, to fill detail voids of understanding and inform both themselves and the related dimensions of a project.

For High Street Heritage we developed an urban strategy for Glasgow's oldest high street through community engagement, anchored by a celebration of the extensive and significant tangible and intangible heritage assets along its length. The New Practice team operates in the same spheres of knowledge common to all those with architectural training, specifically in the realms of heritage architecture and its physical conservation. This knowledge is accompanied similarly by an appreciation for the value and importance of protecting and celebrating these facets of the built environment; however, expert knowledge is required to truly understand the real, wide-ranging social, political and historical context of history within cities and how it impacts people and places. To this end, New Practice collaborated with Dr Alan Leslie on High Street Heritage. Dr Leslie's expertise brought new ways of unpacking and responding to the brief, and acted as a constant challenge to the traditional architectural responses to problems and opportunities encountered throughout the project. Further, having his perspective as a 'heritage litmus test' gave our team the confidence

Heritage walking tour led by Dr Alan Leslie, in collaboration with New Practice for 'Mon the High Street Day', 2021.

that we could perform effectively and professionally, and that the work we were doing was right and good.

Working with Dr Leslie allowed us to incorporate elements of the high street's history that we wouldn't have been aware of, and uncovered stories which became key to the project's narrative. Further, Dr Leslie incorporated his own dark humour, which was possible only from someone who wholly understood the nuance of the topic itself. His walking tours of colloquial heritage on the high street were one of the most successful activities on our key engagement day for the project, to the degree that their future use as a place-making and celebratory prototype was emphasised in our final heritage strategy.

1:100 / Peer: Composition – Visions for Northolt

In Northolt, we recognised the value and need for additional input and perspectives to reach as many people as possible, build genuine connections and bring more people into a space of dialogue in their everyday experience.

Abigail Blunt, Senior Designer, New Practice

In 2021 New Practice was invited to respond to a brief that was heavily anchored in an on-the-ground understanding of the politics surrounding community engagement in Northolt in northwest London. Despite our having carried out work beyond Glasgow already, being based in the city and with our London office not yet established, we quickly recognised that our team lacked a thorough connection to the experience required for such understanding. Having spoken with RESOLVE Collective over video call a number of times during the first wave of the Covid-19 pandemic to understand more about the shared purposes in our practices, we had an opportunity to work together in a context they were already familiar with through their ongoing work with Hawkins\Brown Architects.

The wider context of a design at 1:100 brings the compositional relationship of parts readable with an inhabited human scale into view. The relationship between similarly sized peers forming a full composition is characteristic of this respective scale of collaboration, where the emphasis is on the nature of the human, and the collective of humans, within the composition. Alongside programme and resources, there can be an overwhelming pressure in delivering ambitious work as an emerging practice, which necessitates being able to contribute and benefit from a support system between collaborative peers to produce work which is right and good.

Visions for Northolt 'Summer Event' with RESOLVE Collective in Lime Tree Park.

Adaptive reuse of Kinning Park Complex, completed in 2022 by New Practice.

1:1,000 / People: Place – Redevelopment of Kinning Park Complex

Kinning Park Complex is a building where people meet, learn and collaborate. Its purpose exists as the community has nurtured it over the years to survive – the redevelopment has secured its future for the generations to come.

Racheal Smith, Operations Manager, Kinning Park Complex

Moving beyond individual built works in scale and including a slightly wider context reveals the relationship between the work itself and the local place within which it sits. This incorporation of local context and place is the basis for a scale of collaboration centred upon the culture and concerns of the communities engaging with a project. In the same way that site context informs a more tailored design, working with the myriad voices and perspectives of the urban and cultural fabric of a place fosters the important, nuanced responsiveness and regional particularity of a project.

We consider it imperative to understand the experience of generations past, and engage with neighbours and those who have inhabited local neighbourhoods for a long time. This is especially critical when saving or adapting important civic landmarks for and within communities, in an effort to protect them for future generations. A key need here is the ability to speak candidly and honestly, and engage in difficult conversations about what a community really needs, as opposed to what it really wants – what are its needs for the future in contrast to what it wanted then and what it wants now?

Our work at Kinning Park Complex engaged in this type of collaboration within the community and place. The charity has custodianship over the important, same-named civic building (once an Edwardian school), which has been run as a community centre since the 1990s; it is a highly trusted organisation within its local community. Both charity and client, collaborating with their team on the redevelopment of this civic building, opened up honest conversations about the type of resources and spaces that the people of Kinning Park, historically underserved, need. Working with a community organisation saw us indirectly collaborate with an ever-growing and connected web of local, multi-generational voices from diverse backgrounds. For instance, through connecting to existing outreach programmes taking place in the centre, such as Food Justice Cafe, language classes and repair cafes, to have conversations with their audiences about how the building could better serve their needs, extended the reach of our design and engagement far wider into the community. Further, by approaching our relationship with the locally trusted Kinning Park Complex as a team member, we were able to learn how to best use time and resources to ensure the community was not only engaging with us, but also was comfortable enough to be honest. Anyone can ask questions; the difference is getting honest answers.

1:10,000 / Wider: Learning – Meet Our Waterfront

The scale of opportunity to reconnect Glasgow with its waterfront called for a blended experience, addressing strategic complexities while being nimble on the ground – a positive balance found in our collaboration with New Practice.

Esme Fieldhouse, Head of Public Realm, Hawkins\Brown Architects

Meet Our Waterfront is a project to design a masterplan for a prominent city centre site in Glasgow, on the River Clyde, commonly known as Custom House Quay. The project was led by Hawkins\Brown and Civic Engineers, and New Practice was invited to provide the wide-ranging stakeholder engagement and communications for the

Boat ride discussions underway on the River Clyde for Meet Our Waterfront.

multi-million-pound masterplan. Hawkins\Brown took on a role akin to a mentor, with its wider focus, wealth of experience, operation and context directly informing our own practice and learning during the project. This scale of collaboration can be compared to the scope of a 1:10,000 view, with a more expansive sphere of learning and understanding gained as a wider dimensionality of an entire work and its surrounds comes into focus.

Already mentioned as being critical to successful collaboration, non-extractive and kind relationships were particularly fruitful in our workings on Meet Our Waterfront. Having a lead consultant or lead architect who, like Hawkins\Brown was generous in their want to have more junior team members benefit from a learning experience in their work on the project, meant that we were able to learn from what might be considered stupid questions, or present novel ideas – with no fear of professional disgrace, these often turned into impactful outcomes. Further, our training in architecture means that our perspective on public engagement work (especially when on behalf of another architecture practice) often creates space for inventive dialogue, as we can understand how the data we're gathering can best feed into or evolve concepts into meaningful designs. This in turn makes uniquely design-focused conversation part of the community engagement itself, ultimately making the consultation process stronger. For instance, in discussing the project we kept having conversations about how so few in Glasgow ever get to go on the Clyde itself, it being neither a leisure nor transit-based river for the general public. As a collaborative mentor, Hawkins\Brown was supportive of our novel idea to hire a tugboat and invite members of the public to partake in engagement activities while cruising the length of the river, responding in situ to the emerging vision and ideas for the masterplan.

1:100,000 / Civic: Mosaic – Cambridge Core Site

While the worthwhile space was comparatively small-scale it had the not-so-small task of setting the tone for the wider multi-billion-pound, multi-stakeholder masterplan. We had to ensure that we understood the ambitions of all contributors; distributing work in progress regularly ensured shared threads stitched together the overall vision.

Maeve Dolan, Associate, New Practice

The subject of a pointillist painting, at close quarters an abstract and unrecognisable mass comprising countless flecks of colour, reveals itself as one stands back to view the work in its totality; the same is true of the most expansive scale of collaboration called upon at New Practice. In our commission by U+I and TOWN to write a RIBA Stage 2 feasibility study for a 1.5-hectare worthwhile use in Cambridge, we acted as one tile within the wider civic mosaic of a significantly larger project, both in terms of scale and lifespan. The major multi-billion-pound development of the Cambridge Core Site in northeast Cambridge presented such a monumental scale of change to the built environment, and in such instances it's sometimes hard to understand where genuine collaboration can take place; however, through persevering in an attempt to forge such partnerships, we came to realise that the project is still just a bunch of people trying to make the best work possible. Keeping this perspective allows even the smallest window for the opportunity of teamwork to be seen and seized.

On the project we worked closely with the development manager of TOWN, who was our direct link and critical connection to an intricate and complex

Visualisation of the worthwhile use for the Cambridge Core Site.

web of networks and systems across policy, community, conservation and context. Specific to our facet of the project, this relationship also forged our direct link to the wider teams and present and future stakeholders. Having our own area of concern allowed us to focus time and attention on our work, which was then carefully placed alongside a much broader evolving narrative. Then in much the same manner that TOWN acted as our link in the network, we acted as a further link on its behalf for the numerous teams concerning planning, landscape, infrastructure and sustainability – and in these moments, the flow of knowledge in the collaboration flipped. Ultimately, when concerned with your own tile in the collaborative mosaic, it's often possible to be more detail-focused and have more time and space to reflect on what's right and what's not working.

Each of the scales of collaboration engaged in at New Practice presents its own unique benefit and time for application. However, as in any good design, true richness comes when as many scales as possible are implemented and worked to both a functional and poetic depth across all relevant facets of a project. Consider a refined siting which speaks easily to its topography, or a drip flashing carrying out its function perfectly but fitting effortlessly into the composition of the entire work. The blending and mixing of scales ensures authentic and powerful outcomes, resonating with all collaborators, either directly involved or indirect parties.

This power of collaboration was felt during the pandemic, when work ground to a shuddering halt. We began to think more carefully about how smaller practices of the same scale could genuinely come together, collaborate and compete with larger practices. With two other Glasgow-based practices, O'DonnellBrown and Loader Monteith, we formed a casual group sounding board to start having these conversations on collaboration and resilience – and it's about time we emailed them to arrange a coffee.

Delivering Collaborative Projects

David Ogunmuyiwa, Architecture Doing Place and Karakusevic Carson

Old Peckham Library. Mixed use community and housing collaboration between Architecture Doing Place and Studio Gil – View from existing Estate

The nature of being an architect in practice today requires collaboration. The complexity of the built environment and its enormous common challenges (e.g., the climate crisis, design for social justice, the implementation of new building regulations) require an interdisciplinary approach.

What collaboration looks like is also complex. It is deeply personal and depends on individual personalities, working styles, ethics and values. There is no single formula that our industry can refer to and adopt.

This chapter explores collaboration through the experience of collaborative delivery using the masterplan model, where the masterplanner is a lead architect working with other practices – often smaller – on defined scopes or plots.

It is based on my reflections as the founder of a small practice called ArchitectureDoingPlace and discussions with previous collaborators including Paul Karakusevic, founding partner of Karakusevic Carson Architects (KCA), and Pedro Gil of Studio Gil. KCA is a 100-person practice specialising in regeneration and affordable housing projects for public institutions. Studio Gil is a small studio that has developed a reputation for socially engaged work, listening to and applying the voices of marginalised communities to its projects.

The chapter aims to provide an informal but practical insight into the lessons learned from two sides of architectural practice, large and small.

Although collaborative delivery in the sector of estate regeneration is an old idea (e.g., the work of Darbourne & Darke in the 1960s and 1970s), it seemed to have fallen out of favour with a generation of procurers until recently.

The impetus for collaborative delivery today comes from different impulses, depending on the motivations of a client or collaborator. These motives range from greater inclusion, to accountability of public investment, or improvement of design quality through the heterogeneity of authorship.

For small practices and micro-practices, collaboration is a means of access to larger scales of work or specific sectors; for instance, large estate regenerations for local authorities. In this sector, clients benefit from a diverse design approach through the coordination of a single lead consultant.

The motives for larger practices to collaborate are less obvious. Most have the capacity and resources to act as a 'one-stop shop', delivering big schemes independently and at a competitive price. Larger practices, however, often benefit from collaborative delivery, which demonstrably adds value to projects.

Having struggled to find larger sponsors after founding his practice in 2000, Karakusevic wanted to give the next generation of architects a leg-up.

The collaborative creative process helps the messy early design-oriented process, making it more inclusive for smaller studios that may not yet have the depth of capacity to cope with complex project management demands efficiently.

There is also a mutual benefit. Working with small practices gives architects based in large-scale environments the opportunity to test ideas and assumptions in different working cultures.

Working with smaller practices helps large and medium-sized practices avoid designing on autopilot – repeating the same design response – and offers a new creative challenge and impetus.

The best outcomes result from a design team that includes different voices. Based on Karakusevic's experience as a student at the Royal College of Art, where students were encouraged to work with others from different creative disciplines, KCA prefers that at the beginning of each project, a group of three to four people gather to establish common principles that shape the design approach.

KCA works closely with the other leads in the formative phase of a project to develop common ideas. 'Some of the best projects have been where everyone draws simultaneously – contributing to a equally shared collaboration of ideas.'

This methodology is often an iterative process that highlights individual design priorities and typological experiences. This helps clarify the project vision from the outset and enables a more interesting process with considered design results.

In the later stages of a project, KCA advocates for collaborators to spend time in the physical studios of the lead practice to facilitate an immediate and responsive flow of information. In Karakusevic's experience, smaller practices are sometimes ambivalent about this approach, because of the pressure on their small resources.

Covid-19 affected the way collaborations worked through proximity, but the rapid implementation of digital tools for shared work, namely Zoom, Microsoft Teams, Whiteboard and Conceptboard, helped overcome this.

A common challenge to collaborative delivery is negotiating scopes of work early on. Karakusevic believes

Old Peckham Library. View from new cafe garden

Old Peckham Library. View from Peckham Hill Street

there are even more benefits if collaborators work on the same building on a sub-masterplan project scale and on plots of a masterplan that allow attention to detail on a small and urban scale. However, smaller practices feel this lessens opportunity. The competitiveness between practices to work on prominent or culturally interesting plots on a masterplan is very real; working on a single building therefore might be seen to limit opportunity. Another formula for splitting scope is having no division of scope in the traditional sense, so that collaboration works across every aspect of design, at least in the concept stage. The key to this working is being clear about it at the beginning, but it is again less popular as small practices need to see some architectural manifestation of their collaboration in order to get the benefit of future work.

Collaboration also requires sacrifice for large and medium-sized practices. Without the same capacity or tools, small practices require the help of larger collaboration partners to contribute meaningfully, depending on the scope of work. However, this is delicate, as it is often perceived as simply a grooming of competitive successors. I believe this anxiety is misplaced, as the requirements to lead a large regeneration scheme, such as project management skills, insurance levels, resourcing and robustness, mean that there are distinct and complementary roles for large and small without anyone necessarily stepping on anyone else's toes.

For small practices, the process of working with larger practices is varied and wide-ranging, as lead architects are expected to facilitate collaboration.

Some of the best facilitators of collaboration are large-scale practices with excellent project management capabilities, with the ability to set clear deadlines and boundaries, in addition to sharing templates, systems and interfaces to ensure that all collaborating parties work analogously.

Large practices that account for the size and capacity of small and micro-practices ensure that these teams are protected from the complex project management and resource pressure of working on large-scale projects (especially social housing or regeneration projects) and can therefore focus their efforts on their specific specialities.

ArchitectureDoingPlace, for example, is currently part of a trio of practices working on a 2,000-unit project for a local authority in northeast London. How the collaboration is structured has meant that my practice's unique understanding of estates has given the project a futureproofing aspect. Through spatial proposals and floor plans, we have shown what the project could look like in five years, when maintenance and management budgets are stretched. The result is a project that demonstrates good value for the public purse, and ultimately a project that is more likely to succeed in the long term.

The unique specialisms of small and micro-practices can also afford a wide view over projects and the work of collaborating partners. With an understanding of the needs, wishes and experiences of marginalised and local communities, both my studio and Studio Gil are examples of small practices that provide feedback throughout the design process on topics such as the safety, security and management of estates and the lived experience of residents.

This translates to every level of design, from the location of a pocket park on a large estate that could prove a security risk, to small-scale details such as an openable window shutter, which could become a point of contention between residents and management in terms of maintenance responsibility.

For small practices, the obvious benefit of collaboration is access to larger scales of work or specific sectors. When properly facilitated, it also allows these teams to catapult learning and accelerate processes as specialists, whether social housing experts, regeneration experts or otherwise.

Like Karakusevic, Gil believes that collaboration leads to unexpected solutions that individual teams might not have reached independently: 'The plurality of voices often leads to forward-thinking outcomes, resulting in better and more meaningful projects.'

A common misunderstanding about collaborative delivery is that all stakeholders must always agree on every aspect of the approach at all times. This may seem ideal, but it is through the process of questioning and exploring ideas and the creative tension between collaborators that the approach and ultimately the final result are strengthened.

In practice, it is enjoyable and exciting to contribute our creative ideas and contextual language – verbally and architecturally – to inform a scheme's outcome in large and small ways.

For larger practices with a deeply rooted approach, it is also thrilling to see first-hand how novel it is for these practices to work with nimble design studios. Our references, our representation of ideas and our way of communicating change the way these practices normally work. 'Like a lone creative dribbler tackling his way through a team of defensive midfielders, our presence forces large practices to raise their game by finding novel solutions,' says Gil.

Unlike the best collaborators, who are willing to go on a creative journey together and respect what other parties have to offer to a project, there is still an underlying feeling in some parts of the industry that collaboration is unnecessary and part of a client tick-box exercise. This sensibility is heightened when commissioners realise the benefits of social value by working with different practices much later in the process.

Collaboration is personal and depends on preferred working styles and individual motivations. Understanding and sharing these motivations, in addition to the real drivers for each individual or practice within a collaboration, creates a goal-oriented environment in which everyone involved can strive to achieve, like the client's goals for an inclusive project team.

Where collaborating parties do not heed the advice of smaller practices, it is imperative to be constructively clear about a difference of opinion but not complain from the sidelines. The purpose should always be to make the project better in whatever way, big or small. Not only does this help safeguard reputation if a project-related crisis occurs in the future, but written communication also provides time for reflection for the reader. In my own experience, where I have provided feedback in a workshop or design team meeting that has

View looking through the courtyard garden from Pencraig Way

not been agreed on, it has often been accommodated later in some form after reflection by project leads. Where this didn't happen, at least we felt we tried.

Combined with the challenge of dividing the scope of work, the way design work is credited within collaborations is often precarious for smaller practices. The unique specialities of practices such as Studio Gil and my own cannot be summarised in a simple title. Without the brand recognition of lead architects, there may be little or no recognition or public awareness of our contributions, which add real value to projects. In this way, any worthy attempt by a client to ensure that a project is truly inclusive can be undermined. But this is rare, and I've seen larger practices that don't 'play nice' soon get a reputation for it among smaller practices, who can be influential in other ways.

The revival of the collaborative delivery model over the past five years is the result of the social, political and economic context in which we exist.

Today, the public sector has a huge responsibility to use investments for the greatest public impact and to ensure fair representation and social value. More than ever, the sector is under increased pressure of accountability.

Masterplans and regeneration projects must demonstrate the ability to survive a volatile future, whether from an ecological, environmental or social point of view. Inclusion is incentivised for the benefit of taxpayers. Commissioning diverse practices in terms of size, specialisms and lived experiences can help drive change and remove systemic barriers.

However, for some clients and architectural practices, the opportunity to work together is not just about virtue but primarily about value, by furthering the design ambition and quality of projects. It is also a lucrative way to secure the bottom line of businesses. Many well-established practices today grew by getting access to stable publicly (or part publicly) funded work.

As clients begin to understand the value of collaborative delivery models and look to use them on more and more projects, these models will increase access to large-scale work.

In the current context of economic volatility, such work might be low-margin but stable. Estate regeneration projects are long-term projects, and as we are currently in the midst of a generational housing crisis with a persistent cycle of estate regeneration, these projects provide steady money and public visibility. There is even more potential benefit for large-scale practices. The visibility and validity of leading collaborations on

Ledbury Estate for Southwark Council, Karakusevic Carson Architects. View looking north along Commercial Way

View looking north-west
along Old Kent Road

large public projects increases the opportunity to work on similar projects in the same role. It allows larger practices to demonstrate their own commitment to inclusion on public projects in dense and complex areas with a range of communities.

As this chapter has shown, the challenges for small practices that are part of collaborative delivery models are often greater than those experienced by larger practices. Small and micro-practices such as ArchitectureDoingPlace, Studio Gil and others demonstrate a principle that designers often hold to philosophically – that collaborative delivery models contribute success by making projects better and stronger, serving end users more effectively, and thereby mitigating the risk of wasting investment, carbon and effort.

Here are some key takeaways for all scales of practices to consider:

- 'Play nice' when collaborating with other practices.
- Show humility.
- Understand that the collaboration is often an exchange of value.
- Practise reciprocity in acquisitions.
- Collegiate personalities help.
- Accommodate design process/culture.
- Promote social value and social purpose.
- Client teams need to embrace the spirit too, if it is to work.

Working with large-scale practices as the founder of a small practice on public projects requires a trade-off. To be part of a collaborating team means knowing that the process will sometimes be hard but ultimately successful. As part of this team, beyond access to work, there is a vocational opportunity to share and learn through the lived experience of often completely different communities and minorities. This process provides a granular grounding to some didactic design ideas, while creating a conduit for the voice of stakeholders outside the design process, especially end users.

The relationship can also be reciprocally beneficial. People are good at different things. Different practices of different sizes are suited to different roles in projects. By supporting the capacity of smaller partners, large and medium-sized practices can nurture more robust partners and not simply groom their own successors. As such, it is largely about mindset.

Given the seismic global shifts we have experienced between 2020 and 2022, both politically and socially, it is no longer justified for a monoculture to design environments for all. The greater the plurality of the team, the better the result. If collaborative ways of working can reach their true potential, clients and commissioners can begin to hand over projects to the best types of collaborating teams and, in turn, the built environment will be improved.

ACTIVISM PROFILE

Collective Action in a Climate Emergency

Matthew Morris, Architects Climate Action Network

Architects Climate Action Network, open meeting at the Barbican Centre, London, UK.

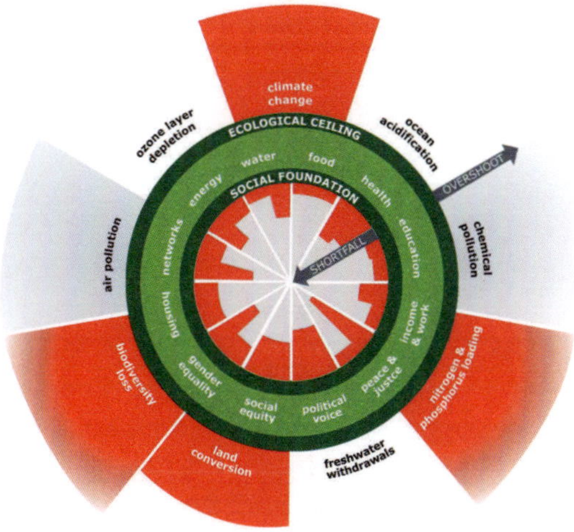

Above: The doughnut of social and planetary boundaries – Kate Raworth, *Doughnut Economics: Seven Ways to Think Like a 21st-Century Economist*, Random House Business, 2018

There is no silver bullet for the world's environmental woes. The climate crisis is unbound by geography, indiscriminate of people, antagonist of systems and uncaring of who or what it may affect, whether directly or indirectly.

The evidence has been mounting for years, and now the race is on to limit the planet's warming to 1.5° C, as set out in the Paris Agreement.[1] Globally, buildings and the construction industry account for 39% of energy-related carbon dioxide (CO_2) emissions.[2]In the UK, it is now legislated that by 2050 emissions will be net zero, yet the built environment and construction sector within the UK is responsible for 40% of the total emissions. Meeting these targets will be challenging.

Systemic change is necessary, and the construction industry needs to undergo a radical cultural transformation and rapid decarbonisation. Deep collaboration, dialogue and pathways towards net zero are needed if we are to remain in a 'safe and just space' – to not overshoot the planetary boundaries and to not fall short on the social foundations of the world.

The Architects Climate Action Network (ACAN) functions as a do-mocracy, meaning that we are practicably acting now for faster and bolder solutions for the built environment – as governing bodies are not doing enough in response to the climate emergency. As a self-supporting network of active individuals within the architecture and related built environment professions, we are driven by three main aims:

- Rapid decarbonisation of the built environment
- Ecological regeneration
- Cultural transformation of the profession

ACAN creates change through:

- Political campaigning and lobbying
- Direct action and public engagement
- Research and knowledge sharing

ACAN was formed in 2019, and is made up of hundreds of grassroots activists. It has published 170 articles, gained over 14,000 followers across social media platforms, presented at over 60 events, including COP26,[3] and formed 10 chapters around the world. As testament to its progress, it is now a B corporation, allowing it to access funding while keeping the self-supporting network in place.

At the core of ACAN's structure is the Coordinators' Circle, consisting of three symbiotic parts: the Thematic Groups, a Steering Group and Core Movement Support.

The Thematic Groups include embodied carbon, circular economy, education, existing buildings, climate literacy and natural materials, and they are responsible for working on the various projects and public-facing campaigns.

Back-of-house operations and logistics are delivered by Core Movement Support, and comprise finance and funding, digital infrastructure and media, and communications and press.

Finally, the Steering Group is focused on the wider strategy and operations of ACAN and consists of solidarity/social values, campaign support, outreach and replication, and events and actions.

The group coordinators from each discipline are responsible for organising the outputs of the group and facilitation. The Coordinators' Circle comes together once a month with each core coordinators' group for an open discussion about ongoing campaigns and projects, to share knowledge and resolve any issues arising.

Architects Climate Action Network, organisation structure.

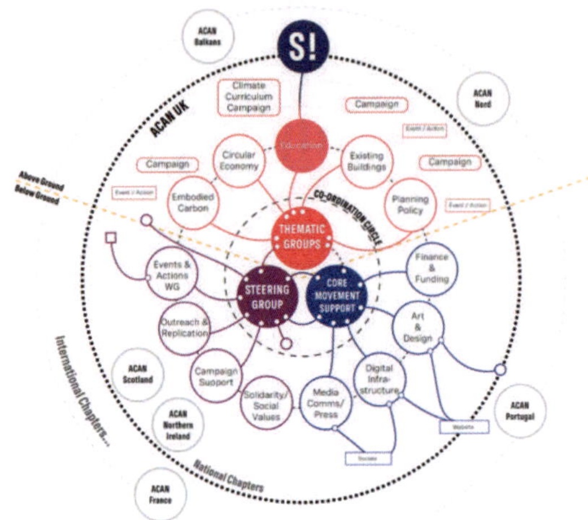

ACAN's work

Regulate Embodied Carbon! campaign

In 2021, ACAN released a report on embodied carbon in the construction sector[4] alongside two briefing notes made available for local authorities and MPs to use. This was largely driven by the independent climate change committee analysis that had identified the need for rapid emissions reduction from the manufacturing and construction industries. Furthermore, it recommended that the government should legislate for embodied carbon assessments and reductions.

The report explained what measures could be adopted by built environment professionals to significantly reduce the embodied carbon within the building sector, and outlined approaches to this. Within the report, several options to regulate embodied carbon from a whole-building perspective, as well as at the individual, material product and component scales, were put forward. This was followed by the identification of six possible phased routes that policymakers, locally and nationally, could start introducing into policy and legislation.

The report and supporting documents were produced and published thanks to a mammoth effort from the authors, contributors, ACAN members, organisation supporters and existing work that others had carried out worldwide. ACAN worked together with these contributors to identify work that already existed with the aim of enhancing and building on it.

Initially, the collaborative efforts sought to map out the UK industry's efforts. We quickly understood that the call to action on embodied carbon measurements and calculations was never based on legislation, and these were only conducted voluntarily, meaning that emissions within the UK are not subject to any

The first reading of the Carbon Emissions Bill in the UK Houses of Parliament by Duncan Baker MP, February 2022.

Architects Climate Action Network, Poster of the Circular Series exhibited at COP26.

regulations and are not covered in the UK planning policies. This focused our attention and adjusted the tone of the work carried out. We subsequently conducted a broader outreach exercise and engaged with counterparts from counties such as Finland and America, where regulatory change is either in process or already realised. As a result of this, we were able to understand the best leverage points and where these regulations would be most suitably placed within the UK legislative framework – in this instance, within building regulations and UK planning policy. The report went out for peer review, and these reviewers in turn became key endorsers.

The Circular Series

Based on the work stages in the RIBA Plan of Work,[5] ACAN's Circular Economy Group devised and delivered a nine-part circular economy online event series focused on understanding how circular economy principles can be applied within the context of the UK construction

Architects Climate Action Network, taking part in the Global Climate Action Strike.

industry. We addressed the key barriers and challenges in adopting circular principles and focused on the opportunities of realising circular approaches throughout a project's life. The series concluded with a newly proposed RIBA stage to close the loop.

Initial discussions with the Circular Economy Group led to the series, and highlighted the momentum circularity was gathering globally – yet with little to no information for its application in the construction industry. We plotted out the various stakeholders, decision-makers and influencers across a project's life cycle and reached out to 18 representative experts from across the industry to address the pertinent stages. Through continuous dialogue and the knowledge that ACAN members had, we recognised that the RIBA work stage scope needed to be extended to facilitate deconstruction and reuse, effectively embedding the circular economy into standard practice.

At each event, open Q&A sessions were held alongside an interactive online 'whiteboard', whereby people could contribute comments and responses to the presentations/discussions. The events were attended by consultants, mechanical, electrical and plumbing (MEP) engineers, structural engineers, architectural technologists, architects, interior designers, planners, contractors and developers. Over 4,000 tickets booked and an ever-growing engagement with the videos that are now online (over 9,000 views) indicates substantial interest for relevant practical information on the subject.

We will be launching a Circular Construction Reference Guide based on data collected during the series; at the time of writing this is out for consultation with industry collaborators prior to publication.

Creating change

Despite slow movement from the construction industry, we have demonstrated our ability to adapt. There is the appetite for change, and it is time to evolve again by responding to the climate emergency – harnessing technological, environmental and economical design solutions, addressing the science and meeting the demands for the future. It is imperative that built environment professionals take immediate action.

For too long, we have practised in a manner that has blatantly degraded our planet and is contributing significantly to the climate emergency. The opportunity is explicit: a chance to assemble around a common goal; to respond not with a silver bullet but a golden thread woven by deep collaboration and ongoing dialogue that will develop the skills, enable the capacity and share the responsibility. All of these are required to meet the 2050 climate targets.

1 United Nations Climate Change, 'What is the Paris Agreement?', https://unfccc.int/process-and-meetings/the-paris-agreement/the-paris-agreement (accessed 19 September 2022).
2 World Green Building Council, 'New report: The building and construction sector can reach net zero carbon emissions by 2050', 23 September 2019, https://www.worldgbc.org/news-media/WorldGBC-embodied-carbon-report-published (accessed 19 September 2022).
3 https://ukcop26.org/ (accessed 19 September 2022).
4 ACAN, 'The carbon footprint of construction', February 2021, https://www.architectscan.org/_files/ugd/b22203_c17af553402146638e9bc877101630f3.pdf (accessed 19 September 2022).
5 RIBA, Plan of Work, https://www.architecture.com/knowledge-and-resources/resources-landing-page/riba-plan-of-work (accessed 19 September 2022).

ACTIVISM PROFILE

Changing the Narrative for Collective Impact

Lanre Gbolade, Paradigm Network

Paradigm Network committee members, from left to right: Ushma Samani, Tara Gbolade, Lanre Gbolade, Diana Yu, Yemí Aládérun.

Paradigm Network was founded in 2017 by Chris Nasah, Lanre Gbolade, Roberston Lindsay, Tara Gbolade and Yemí Aládérun. The network is run by a committee, which includes Diana Yu, Ushma Samani and a number of the co-founding members.

We believe the breadth of professional expertise and experience within the committee and advisers enables the network to acutely pinpoint and facilitate activities that address the present-day challenges under-represented ethnic groups face within the built environment (BE) industry. All of us operate in the BE industry with a bias towards the practice of architecture but also bringing experience covering public and private client-side roles, design management, development management and strategic consulting. Through our collective experiences in the industry, spanning more than 70 years, we know the power of effective collaborative working to deliver truly impactful change.

Although established on inception as an informal social enterprise, we've grown significantly in the intervening period to over 1,000 people in our network. We are now moving towards formal establishment as a Community Interest Company, which will enable the progression of a resilient growth and transition strategy over the coming years, as well as supporting our aims and objectives through grant funding opportunities.

What is the Paradigm Network?

The Paradigm Network is a forum for BE professionals and students who are passionate about increasing Black and Asian representation within the construction industry. Our strength is in working in collaboration across the professional pipeline. We exist to support, encourage and help talented students and practitioners from Black and Asian backgrounds in education and as they progress in their careers. We place strategic importance on promoting the development of Black and Asian-led practices, challenging perceptions that they don't exist within the UK built environment.

Fundamentally, we exist to be a beacon of hope, inspiration and support to Black and Asian BE professionals and students, having a generational impact for decades to come.

The network provides a platform for Black and Asian students and professionals within the BE industry to network, connect, and share knowledge and experiences that ultimately support their growth in education and their careers. We place strategic importance on elevating and giving visibility to Black- and Asian-led practices and individuals, showcasing their successes and talent. Our website hosts a growing page, promoting high-quality architecture practices, for potential clients and partners to find professionals and support the change in the industry. Our social media content aligns to inspire

Paradigm Network 2019 Alternative Architect event, showcasing different career opportunities for architects beyond traditional practice.

the network's younger student members through the successes and possibilities while also promoting the achievement of professional members.

We also create safe spaces to unwind and relax through a calendar of social events where less experienced members of the group can meet with colleagues at a similar stage in their careers and also establish networks with senior professionals and Black/Asian practice directors and associates for informal chats, guidance and mentoring.

With the collaborative support of our Partner Practices and sponsors, we host a range of online webinars, CPD-style presentations and provocative talks to inspire the network. These events also serve to educate, inform and encourage members, who often share the racial and discriminatory barriers they face in university education, which often also translate into the workplace.

Why Paradigm?

Some people within the BE professions may question why a forum like Paradigm needs to exist, irrespective of the obvious reasons associated with societal racism and discrimination. If that wasn't already apparent, hopefully the powerful Black Lives Matter movement from 2020 has brought to clearer light the fact that architecture and the built environment are not immune to racism, and that this is an issue we need to address for the betterment of society.

In the AJ100 2020 survey,[1] Black architects were found to be 'hugely under-represented'. This has been supported by the ARB

(Architects Registration Board) Equality and Diversity (E&D) survey data,[2] as of January 2022, which shows that 0.9% of registered architects in the UK are Black/Black British and 7% are Asian or Asian British in a country where 20% of the population is from an ethnic minority. By contrast 82% of architects are classified as white. We'd be also interested to drill down further into more granular, intersectional data such as the percentage of Black/Indian Asian women architects, where we suspect the figure is a drop in the ocean. This needs to change.

Diversity data clearly shows the lack of ethnic representation in the architecture profession, but we also have to consider the intersectional discussions associated with social class, affluence and privilege that architecture traditionally combines and uses against those who don't fit the stereotypes. The AJ Race Diversity Survey 2020[3] provides pretty stark details of some of the experiences faced by Black and Asian practitioners. It's little wonder then that many practitioners feel they hit a glass ceiling very quickly in organisations where they are seen as 'other'.

The hard-hitting reality behind these figures is the challenging lived experience of many Black and Asian architects and students that is a result of the structural privilege cemented into the architectural landscape in the UK. Being frank, Black and Asian professionals leading practices will often tell us of the difficulties they face in sustaining a living practising their vocation, and of having limited visibility of opportunities that their white counterparts tend to find it easier to come by.

These statistics have been evident for many years, and alongside the co-founding members' personal professional experience of discrimination, racism and hitting glass ceilings, this gave us the impetus to take action and establish a safe space in which to have challenging conversations, with the beneficiaries being not only Paradigm Network members but also our partners and collaborators.

Above: Paradigm Network professional development seminar.

Below: Paradigm Network CPD and networking event.

Black Lives Matter definitely brought the discussion around prejudice, discrimination and racism to the fore in all fields and industries on a global level, but probably more so in architecture and the discussions around the creation of the built environment, which must be viewed through the lens of being a worthy pursuit fundamentally based on social justice and inclusion.

Through our work at Paradigm we are seeing signs of inclusivity and diverse representation improving within the UK industry, especially in procurement processes promoting genuine collaboration opportunities and diverse project teams. However, with the hard data still showing comparatively low ethnicity statistics overall in the professions that shape our physical landscapes and built forms, can the industry proudly stand up and say it truly serves society?

For the Paradigm committee, diversity matters for three main reasons (and a host of others):

1. It makes the profession more sustainable, current and stronger in depth. It brings those marginalised and unrepresented groups into the fold and enables fresh perspectives and life experiences to shape projects, practices, the profession and built environment industry for the betterment of society as a whole.

2. As an example, the drop-out rate of Part 1 to Part 2 for Black male students is around 50%, according to the AJ's 2019 Student Survey.[4] The RIBA's Education Statistics survey from 2018/19[5] also showed that while 8.3% of students applying to study architecture described themselves as Black, only 1.5% of those students successfully went on to complete their architectural education. Whether prior to starting formal architectural training or entering the workplace, there's a need for future members of the industry and profession to actually see and interact with a diverse pool of actors in the industry (specifically, more people of colour like themselves and with similar cultural backgrounds), and especially operating at senior management level.

3. It actually just makes sustainable business sense! From a purely selfish perspective, you might expect business leaders to think about the bottom line a bit more acutely. Workplace performance research has also repeatedly shown that more diverse workplaces and company boards are more likely to deliver high performance

Paradigm on-site building tours, led by partner practices and organisations.

and returns compared to those with a less diverse make-up. In fact, McKinsey's 2020 'Diversity wins' report[6] stated that 'Our latest analysis reaffirms the strong business case for both gender diversity and ethnic and cultural diversity in corporate leadership – and shows that this business case continues to strengthen. The most diverse companies are now more likely than ever to outperform less diverse peers on profitability. Moreover, we found that the greater the representation, the higher the likelihood of outperformance.' It really is that simple.

How we're changing the narrative for a wider collective impact

We encourage more diverse client and design teams, reflecting the society we live in to create a richer and enhanced built environment. We do this through activism and lobbying within the profession around education and career progression, strategic thinking with national and international organisational bodies, and collaborative work with industry supporters.

We support and help develop talented architects from diverse backgrounds in their education and as they progress in their careers through knowledge-sharing in the network. This takes place through informal mentoring as well as more structured collaborative partnerships with our partner organisations.

We are a collaborative bridge between the profession and public organisations by arranging and curating industry-related workshops, presentations and outreach programmes focused on supporting minoritised group initiatives and the application of best-practice principles.

We integrate fully the contributions of Black and Asian professionals as providers of architecture and design services. We are strategic in creating visibility for this particular group and celebrate their contribution to the profession and society by providing a mutually beneficial platform between the marginalised and the mainstream.

Over the last two years we have seen rapid growth in our membership and partnerships with national institutions and industry professionals. We have attracted funding and received media coverage within the architectural profession. Members have achieved successes in completing architectural education, and have secured work placements, architectural roles and job promotions thanks to support received via the network. Other unquantifiable measures of success that are key to our mission include the growth of personal confidence and impact reported by our members. These initial successes have given us confidence as a committee that we're making inroads and making a difference, but there is lots more to do.

We welcome anyone who wants to join us on this journey in the struggle for a more diverse and just built environment that serves us all.

1 Bruce Tether, 'AJ100 2020: Can architects recover the optimism they had in our pre-Coronavirus survey?', *Architects' Journal*, 1 June 2020, https://www.architectsjournal.co.uk/news/aj100-2020-can-architects-recover-the-optimism-they-had-in-our-pre-coronavirus-survey (accessed 19 September 2022).
2 ARB (Architects Registration Board) Equality and Diversity (E&D) Survey data.
3 Richard Waite, 'Architecture is systemically racist. So what is the profession going to do about it?', *Architects' Journal*, 23 July 2020, https://www.architectsjournal.co.uk/news/architecture-is-systemically-racist-so-what-is-the-profession-going-to-do-about-it (accessed 26 September 2022).
4 AJ Student Survey 2019: the harsh realities of life in practice.
5 RIBA Education Department Statistics Survey 2018/19.
6 McKinsey & Company, 'Diversity wins: How inclusion matters', May 2020, https://www.mckinsey.com/~/media/mckinsey/featured%20insights/diversity%20and%20inclusion/diversity%20wins%20how%20inclusion%20matters/diversity-wins-how-inclusion-matters-vf.pdf (accessed 19 September 2022).

ACTIVISM PROFILE

An Inclusive Way Forward: An Activist's Perspective

Amy Francis-Smith

Birmingham Architectural Association, International Women's Day Event, Birmingham, 2019. Vice-President Amy Francis-Smith delivering a talk on diversity, inclusion and representation in the construction industry.

Before the inclusive design movement started to build momentum, access issues were seen as just another tokenistic gesture tacked on to the end of the design process; another annoying and seemingly restricting set of rules laid out in Building Regulations (Part M: Access)[1] which dampened creativity and design innovation.

The general perception was that if you'd ticked the standard ramp, lift and loo box then you'd done your duty towards disabled people. A comparison can be made with the eco architecture movement 20 years ago, where a green roof and some solar panels equated to a sustainable building. We all know that applying a plaster rather than addressing the root issue is pointless, and that a deeper, more integrated approach is required to solve systemic problems.

Inclusive design, now one of the RIBA's core CPD topics,[2] doesn't stem from dry, prescriptive guidance documents. The underlying principles are core to why we design, and why we craft beautiful spaces – because inclusive design really just means allowing every person to enjoy and to fully inhabit our world.

Access consultancy appears to be a niche specialism: another fringe adviser infrequently making an appearance in a design team meeting to throw a regulatory spanner in the works of an already complex project. But it shouldn't be down to an access consultant to make a scheme inclusive; architects have been trained, and are responsible for envisaging potential clients and designing to their needs.

For centuries our built environment, both consciously and subconsciously, has actively excluded and discriminated whole swathes of society. The spaces we have designed and the structures we have built have created physical segregation and literal tiered societies. There are many examples of how architecture has had a negative impact on different groups of people, but disabled people are most directly affected.

My work and research over the last decade or so has been dominated by the interplay of architecture and provisions for people across the spectrum of disability. Too frequently, people associate disability purely with wheelchair users, no doubt reinforced by the disabled symbol.

Wheelchair users and those with mobility issues are just one part of a much wider demographic, including those with hearing, visual or cognitive impairments, mental health and learning difficulties, neurodiversity, memory concerns or reduced dexterity. In the UK, the disabled community consists of 14.1 million people,[3] the largest minority, making up 19% of the population.[4]

Disability can also come to any one of us at any time. Although it is uncomfortable to consider the fragility of the human condition, it is worth remembering that eight out of 10 disabled people were not born

International Symbol of Access, ISO 7001. The wheelchair user symbol is universally recognised as representing disability; however, it has meant that people with other types of disability aren't always as visible in the public psyche.

that way but acquired a disability during their life.[5] All too regularly, people do not realise how difficult it is to navigate an ableist world until they or a loved one are forced to re-evaluate this.

Considering the vast numbers of people affected, a disabled perspective is so rarely heard; we always talk of providing for the disabled, rather by the disabled. The slogan 'nothing about us without us',[6] originated by disability rights activists, calls for policy and interactions to involve people directly.

The disabled community are tirelessly vocal; follow certain Twitter threads and you will realise that thousands of people are frustrated, trapped and demanding change. They are no longer willing to accept the pitying and patronising handouts, a hangover from the charitable institutions for the 'poor cripples'.[7] Unfortunately, as in all echo chambers, they tend to be preaching to the choir.

I realised I could use my privilege and unique position as an architect to address some of the key issues disabled people face in the built environment. With insights into the construction industry and a platform that spanned multiple sectors, I could potentially enact real change. I hoped that even if I influenced just one person to reconsider their design or bring up the topic in a meeting, someone's life might eventually be improved as a result.

My own personal experiences have greatly influenced my practice; I have lived with intermittent wheelchair use and partial hearing loss due to extensive surgeries since childhood. I vividly remember having to be escorted around the outside of my school in the rain to get to classes, as the single-storey building had multiple flights of stairs but no lifts.

I also acted as a carer for my mother, a crutches and wheelchair user, and we would regularly have to drag her across gravel paths and cobbled streets. If sat before a step at the front of a building, we would often be redirected through a side door, past bins and loading bays, rather than using the main entrance with everyone else. It is worth noting that the Equality Act 2010[8] has brought improvements; however, many buildings are still not compliant or meeting their legal duty for 'reasonable adjustments'.

As an adult, I became suddenly and extremely ill partway through my Master's. I spent the next few years having almost daily anaphylaxis, multiple near-death experiences, periods of being bedridden and hospitalised; balancing a very fine line to manage just simple daily tasks. Diagnosed with the rare condition Mast Cell Activation Syndrome,[9] as well as Crohn's and Ehlers-Danlos Syndrome, I was forced to give up almost every part of my life.

My fight to regain some semblance of health also ignited a flame within me to fight the injustices that other people face. I knew of so many people suffering and struggling in situations not too dissimilar from my own.

Amy Francis-Smith,
NHS Toilet Critique, 2019.

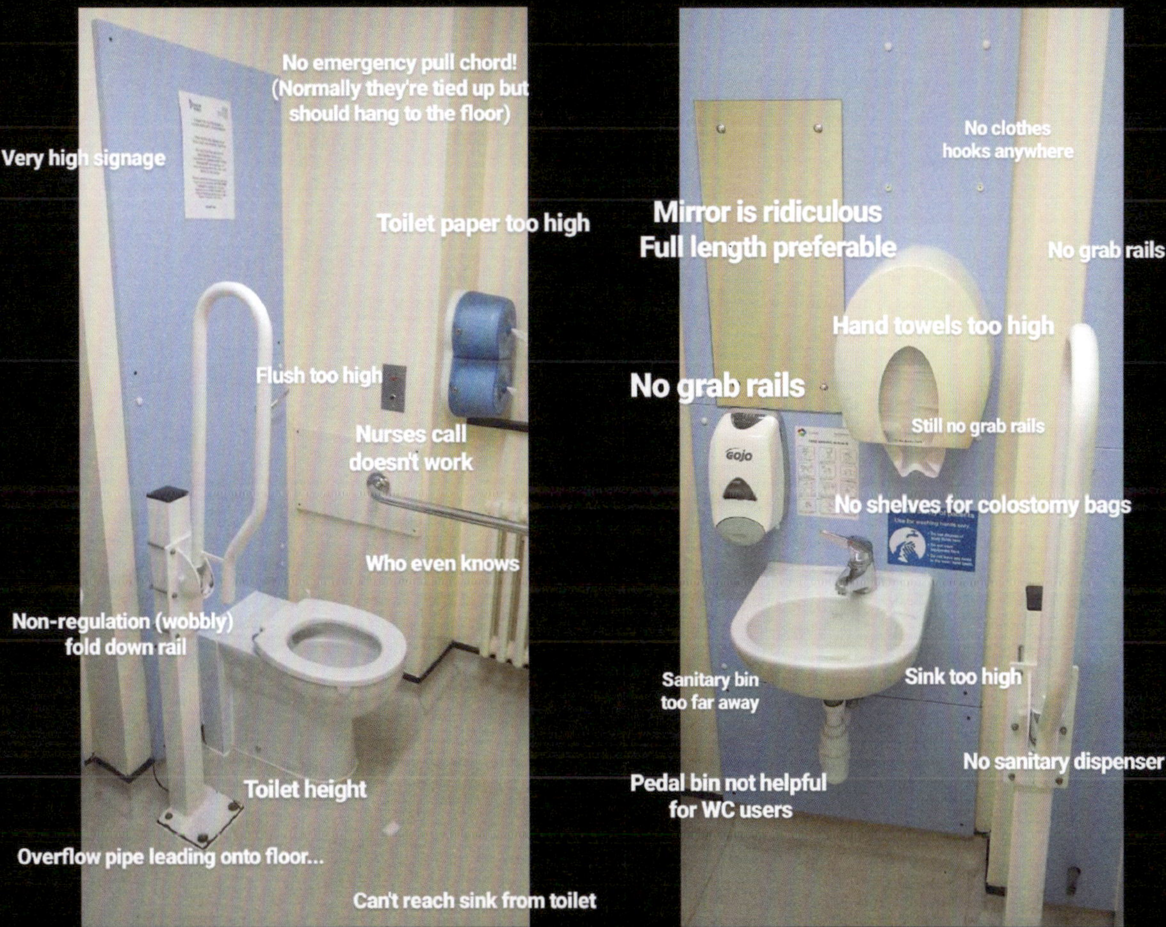

MODERN ACTIVISM

WITH SOPHIE WALKER

'1.8 million disabled people are stuck in houses where they feel imprisoned'

In our regular column, Sophie Walker, feminist campaigner and author of *Five Rules For Rebellion: Let's Change The World Ourselves*, spotlights women fighting for change. This week, she talks to Amy Francis-Smith, 30, an architect based in Birmingham who advocates for inclusive design.

Amy Francis-Smith

Hello Amy, can you tell us about what you do?
I work in the construction industry, which is predominantly white and male. Yesterday, I was in a meeting with 14 men – there were more men called Simon than women in that room! Right now, my work focuses on providing accessible accommodation and provisions for people with disabilities and the elderly.

You must really want to be in that room! Why?
I got into architecture because I wanted a challenge. This work is rational but also creative. Growing up, I had health issues and was in a wheelchair on and off. My hearing was affected and I've got the rare condition Mast Cell Activation Syndrome (which prompts allergic symptoms like anaphylaxis), as well as Crohn's disease and Ehlers-Danlos Syndrome (which causes dislocated joints and organ issues) that forced me to leave university and quit my job.

Scan to visit amyfrancissmith.com

How did that experience ignite your passion for architecture?
At school I couldn't get up or down stairs so I had to be escorted around the outside of the building, often in the rain. My mum also uses a wheelchair intermittently and, as a carer for her, I had to help her navigate kerbs and wait forever for a bus that could fit her wheelchair. A neighbour had motor neurone disease and I saw how the council advised them to install all of these adaptations that really devalued and ruined their family home. Inspired, I drew up sketches for an adapted layout.

How does this passion translate into your work?
The turning point for me was doing a research paper on accessible housing. I discovered there are 14.1 million disabled people in the UK, with 1.8 million stuck in inaccessible housing. Only 9% of houses have even the most basic access features. That really shook me. People are stuck in places where they feel imprisoned, where they can't wash except in the kitchen or can't put their kids to bed because they can't get upstairs. I now work for an architecture firm that specialises in healthcare and residential projects and I'm an access consultant who can advise on design.

How does that translate into campaigning work?
I lobby the Government and increase public awareness to improve legislation and provisions for accessible housing. I also give training to students and professionals to help them realise this is not just a legal but a social responsibility. Something they might think is minor can have major implications for other people's lives.

How can *Grazia* readers support the work you're doing and your campaign?
Find me on Twitter and Insta on @amyfrancissmith or visit my website: amyfrancissmith.com. Check out Habinteg, who I work with and their #ForAccessibleHousing campaign (habinteg.org.uk/fah). I'd encourage disabled people and anyone who feels they are not represented in the construction, design and planning industries to get involved. And for everyone: if day to day you notice that a shop is inaccessible or a lift is out of order – question the shopkeeper, or write to your MP. At work, ask your director how you can build an inclusive workplace. Because you can't do that if people can't even get through the door.

Through my research[10] I have spoken to hundreds of disabled people who recurringly feel trapped, isolated and imprisoned; unable to do daily tasks we take for granted such as opening a window or putting their kids to bed; or having to wash themselves in the kitchen sink because they can't access their bathroom.

Only 7% of UK housing meets the most basic access requirements. If all the accessible housing was condensed into the same area, this would equate to the residences in just 12 of the 32 London boroughs. Thankfully, in August 2022 the UK government finally agreed to increase the accessibility standards for all newbuild homes.

In our modern world, it is somehow still socially acceptable to quite literally segregate and discriminate because of historic building fabric and human-made structures. Everyone deserves autonomy, independence, dignity and respect; human-made disabling structures have been designed in, so they can be designed out just as easily.

As an individual activist and campaigner it's been pretty lonely out there at times, shouting my message into the ether, hoping it might make a small impact somewhere.

I use social media to find like-minded people, engage with the community, share resources, highlight negatives and offer potential solutions.

Using social media has been an effective way to highlight poorly thought-out and inaccessible spaces in the built environment. Visual representation and a comedic casual tone help people to understand the importance of access in more relatable way, and to see beyond the dry requirements of the Building Regulations.

I reached out to professionals on LinkedIn, took myself to conferences and spoke to people already on the scene. The people who I once admired as 'influencer activists' are now my allies and co-campaigning experts in the field, all working collectively towards the same aim.

The small incremental actions progressed and eventually built some real momentum that would not have been possible had I done it alone.

Tackling the injustice requires a multi-pronged strategy, and I've found it important to talk to people at all different levels and backgrounds to seed the idea. Top-level legislative reform and government policy is key for an overarching national implementation, but it trickles down to planning departments and housing developers, educating professionals about their social responsibility and working with universities to embed inclusive design into the curriculum.

Collaborating with journalists and alternative media outlets has brought the message beyond the realms of the construction/architecture industry and into the public domain. Working with

***Grazia* UK, 'Modern activism' interview with Sophie Walker, 2021. Alternative, non-typical forms of media are key to spread the message beyond the architecture industry. The *Grazia* magazine article reached a much more diverse readership, with a call to action that inspired others to become changemakers.**

publications and organisations such as the BBC, CITY A.M.,[11] *Grazia*[12] and the *Financial Times*[13] has helped to make wider society aware of the current issues and ways they too could get involved.

Ultimately my aim is to bring more empathy into design, and promoting quite minor considerations can genuinely make big improvements to people's lives; the basic design principles really aren't rocket science.

I would also like to encourage more disabled architects into the industry, as we need more designers who can make valuable contributions and offer alternative perspectives towards innovation. The route to accreditation is notoriously arduous at the best of times, but for disabled students the barriers are plentiful. As it is, the long working hours put an intense strain on people's health, so if you weren't ill before, the stress will eventually catch up with you.

I was once told, while very ill, by a tutor that if I 'couldn't handle the stress of architecture school' then I'd never cut it in industry, so I should 'go and do something like graphic design instead'. These attitudes are unhelpful and reinforce the idea that architecture is only for those who are physically and mentally strong enough to handle the intense pressure.

Inclusive design is inherently collaborative, and without the acts of talking, workshopping and engaging with others beyond our own lived experience, we risk remaining in our bubble with narrow viewpoints. The same old faces produce the same old spaces.

I get tired of hearing people complain about an issue, but making no effort themselves to change it. You don't have to save the world – start small, start local, but take action! Find your people, those who are just as passionate about whatever battle it is you want to address, and soon the collective energy will have a compounding effect.

'Nothing about us without us' banner, People's History Museum, 2015. The slogan 'nothing about us without us' is often used by disabled people to highlight that no decision should be made without involving the members of the group who might be affected by that decision. Disabled people don't want things imposed on them without consultation and recognition that their opinions, informed by lived experience, are valuable.

Birmingham Design Festival, 'Nothing about us without us'. Amy Francis-Smith talking at Birmingham Design Festival's 2022 event, discussing disability and ways to design our world more inclusively. It covered topics such as societal inequality, user-led design and subtle integrations, and started with disability as an exciting driver for a brief – considering not just our physical realm but the ever-expanding digital space, where accessibility is just as important.

1 GOV.UK, 'Access to and use of buildings: Approved Document M', https://www.gov.uk/government/publications/access- to-and-use-of-buildings-approved-document-m (accessed 25 March 2022).
2 RIBA, 'CPD core curriculum topic: Inclusive Environments', https://www.architecture.com/education-cpd-and-careers/cpd/cpd-core-curriculum/inclusive-environments (accessed 25 March 2022).
3 GOV.UK, 'Family resources survey: Financial year 2019 to 2020', https://www.gov.uk/government/statistics/family-re sources-survey-financial-year-2019-to-2020/family-resources-survey-financial-year-2019-to-2020 (accessed 25 March 2022).
4 Ibid.
5 Purple, 'An overview of disability – infographic', https://wearepurple.org.uk/an-overview-of-disability-infographic/ (accessed 25 March 2022).
6 James I Charlton, *Nothing About Us Without Us*, University of California Press, 2000.
7 John G Richardson and Justin JW Powell, *Comparing Special Education: Origins to Contemporary Paradoxes*, Stanford University Press, 2011.
8 Equality Act 2010, https://www.legislation.gov.uk/ukpga/2010/15/conte nts (accessed 25 March 2022).
9 American Academy of Allergy, Asthma and Immunology, 'Mast Cell Activation Syndrome (MCAS)', https://www.aaaai.org/conditions-treatments/related-conditions/mcas (accessed 23 September 2022).
10 Amy Francis-Smith, 'Psychogeography of the home – a disabled perspective: A contextualised analysis of the UK accessible housing market', MArch Master of Architecture, Birmingham City University, 2019, https://issuu.com/amyfrancis-smith/docs/psychogeog raphy_of_the_home_-_amy_f (accessed 25 March 2022).
11 Elena Siniscalco, 'London is failing to make itself more accessible for those with disabilities', CITY A.M, 2 November 2021, https://www.cityam.com/disability-workplace-access -inclusivity-architecture/ (accessed 25 March 2022).
12 Sophie Walker, 'Modern activism', *Grazia* UK, 29 November 2021, p69.
13 Camilla Bell-Davies, 'Can architecture improve the lives of chronic pain sufferers?', *FT Weekend*, 8 January 2022, https://www.ft.com/content/3480da3f-d029-4c9d-a552 -ce09c07d4e62 (accessed 25 March 2022), p8.

'Can architects make a difference?', Archiboo and the Royal Academy for London Festival of Architecture, 2022. As part of the LFA's Architecture Symposium Debate, panellists Charlie Edmonds, Amy Francis-Smith, Dr Penny Lewis, Amrita Mahindroo, Joe Morris and chair Kunle Olulode discussed the wider impact architects can have in society. Each brought their own specialism and background to an informed, lively discussion.

PRACTICE CASE STUDY

Building Housing to Build Community

La Borda
Lacol

Opposite: La Borda, Barcelona, 2018. La Borda's south facade seen from the future park of Can Batlló.

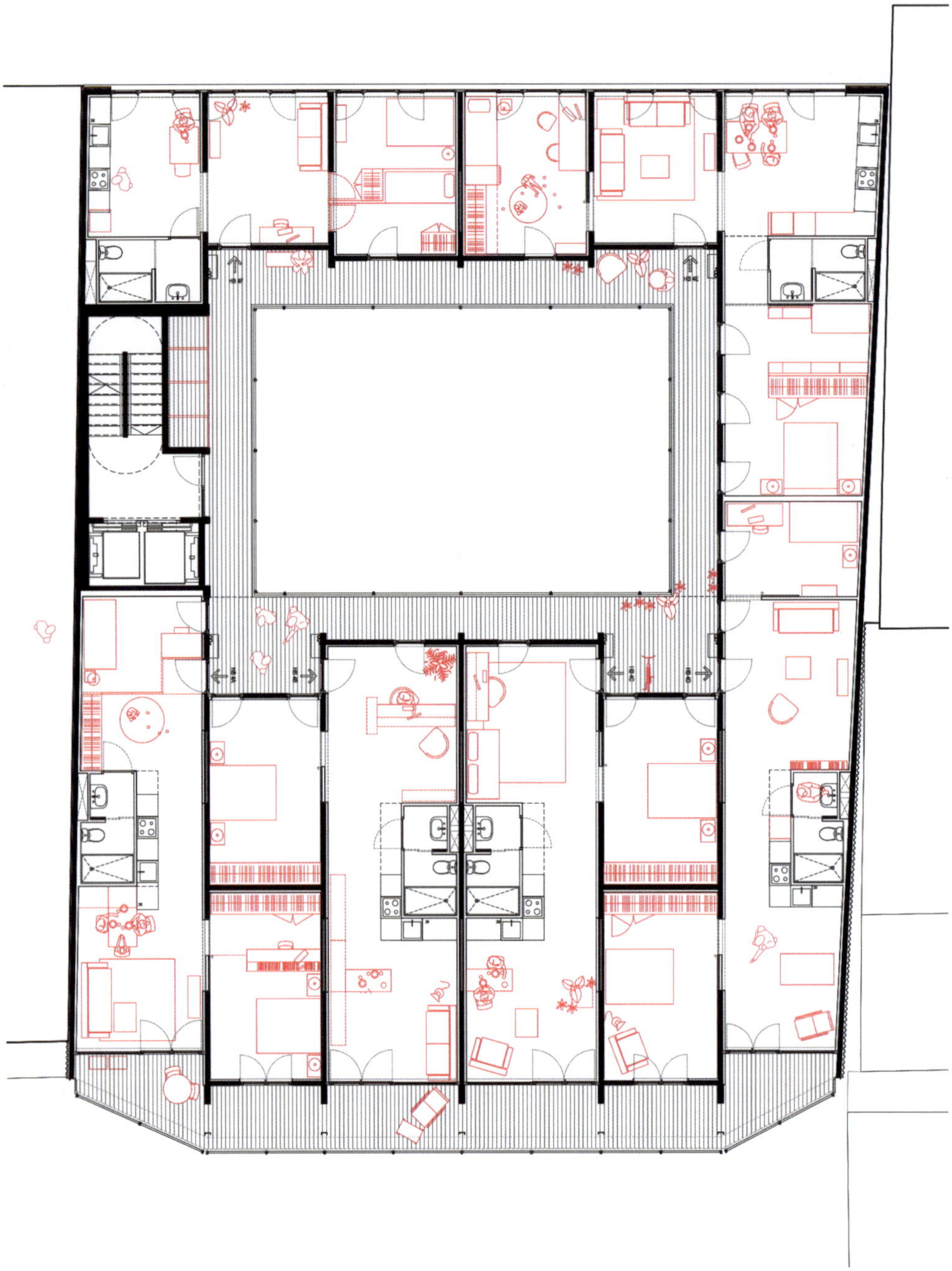

La Borda, Barcelona, 2018. Plan of the fourth floor. Houses were handed over once baseline habitational requirements were met, after which each cohabitating unit could decide how and when to add the finishing touches they deemed necessary. After residents were assigned housing, specific adaptations arose during the development phase within functional and regulatory limits.

In many societies, access to housing is approached individually, as single occupancy or part of a reduced nucleus of cohabitation that includes first-degree relatives. These nuclei are getting smaller, and the number of people living alone is also increasing, reinforcing a degree of isolation that pushes our cities towards individualism and loneliness. In addition, homeownership is seen as a financial asset. As a result, housing is becoming increasingly unaffordable in cities worldwide. None of this comes from natural human desire, but is instead the result of decades of public policies, in addition to commercial endeavours by banks and companies.

However, we are also witnessing a resurgence of cooperative housing movements similar to those seen in the movement's initial wave in the early 20th century and its expansion in the 1970s. Nestled among this wave of new projects, La Borda began in 2012. As part of the local community takeover of the former Can Batlló factory, a group of residents decided to get together to collectively resolve the need for access to housing.

Lacol has been involved from the beginning, viewing it as an opportunity to rethink accessible housing development. La Borda's commitment to a community-based self-development model has made it possible to overcome some existing limitations seen in conventional developments: the fear of the future resident, who is completely unknown, and the market 'mediocratisation' of housing as an item for consumption. Different characteristics of the innovative development process have been key to moving beyond merely formal design questions.

Below: La Borda, Barcelona, 2018. Cooperative members and future residents have been involved in the management, control and accomplishment of the entire development process, through an internal structure that encourages their direct participation, with working committees and a monthly general assembly.

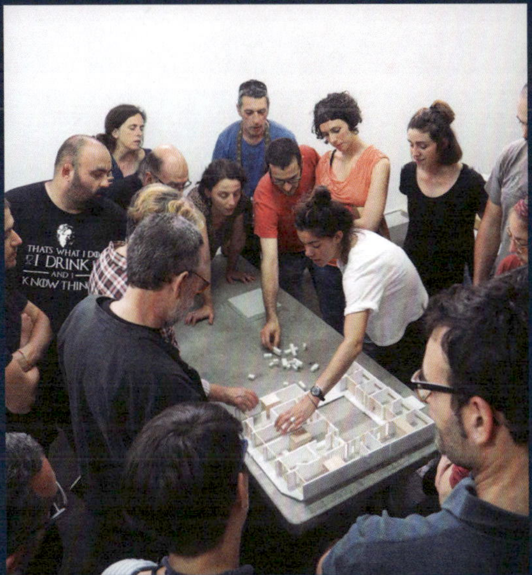

Self-development

The involvement of future residents, usually a great unknown in all collective housing projects, was the project's starting point. A thorough knowledge of each future resident and their real needs and the active participation of residents has been present in all phases: design, construction and management of the building. Participation was channelled through thematic workshops that harnessed the collective intelligence of the group. This process increased awareness and expertise, and stimulated a sense of community and belonging.

Grant-of-use, collective ownership, flexibility and adaptability

The cooperative owns the building, built on a publicly owned plot of land intended for social housing, and assigns residential right-of-use to its members. Hence, the building was conceived as an open structure, the use of which is what ultimately shapes the architecture, adapting to the evolution of the community and the changing needs of residents. The management of the building is taken on by the community itself.

The common infrastructure (support) is a grid of rooms (16m²), allowing for a non-hierarchical type of housing that can be adapted by each resident. In anticipation of future changes, the structure is prepared so that some spaces can be ceded from one house to another through a simple physical and legal operation.

Opposite: La Borda, Barcelona, 2018. Multipurpose room on the first floor. This space has been claimed by the children as their playground. The washing machines will be separated in the future works.

Below: La Borda, Barcelona, 2018. Entrance to the communal kitchen–dining room, seen from the courtyard. This space hosts a weekly communal dinner where everyone in the building is invited to participate. The rest of the days can be booked for internal meetings or personal events of the members.

Community life

La Borda seeks to boost, through common space, community-based housing models that enhance residents' interrelationships, and to establish cooperational ties in the areas of domestic work and care by rendering the private spheres of daily life visible. Here almost 25% of the floor area is given over to common spaces, while in conventional multi-family buildings it is typically calculated to 10% and limited to circulation. There is an 80 m² communal kitchen–dining room, a 100 m² covered multipurpose space, two guest rooms, a laundry room, a large central circulation space, bicycle parking and outdoor terraces.

These community spaces serve a triple purpose: as a meeting place to strengthen relationships; to improve efficiency, avoiding multiplying certain elements across all 28 homes; and to increase the usable floor area for all members, who have access to considerably more space than in a conventional development with the same total floor area and cost.

We rethink collective housing planning to adapt it to the life model conceived of by future residents, breaking with the paradigm of the building as a sum of its individual units, and appreciating it as a single shared house in which the boundary between private and community space is blurred.

LLIBERTAT
PRESOS
POLÍTICS!

Above: La Borda, Barcelona, 2018. A greenhouse covers the courtyard. This is the only automated part of the building, with wind, sun, heat sensors and smoke detectors that regulate the opening of the greenhouse and the sunshade.

Opposite: La Borda, Barcelona, 2018. The covered courtyard was implemented not only for its climatic functions – it was proposed by the community from the early design stage as a way to recover the corralas, old patios found in central and southern Spain, and a typology often used in housing.

Sustainability

The cooperative prioritised the achievement of minimal environmental impact both in construction and in use, and to eliminate the risk of energy poverty among residents. The strategic starting point of the project was to reduce energy demand, as well as finding solutions involving the active participation of residents in the climatic management. The result is a close-to-zero net energy consumption rate, with comfort in the home therefore coming with only the minimum associated cost.

The first important decision was to avoid the construction of an underground car park. There is a direct consequence of this in the construction and use of the building and, in addition, this strategy provides a clear boost to sustainable mobility and the reduction of residents' environmental footprint. Also, the six-storey structure is made of cross-laminated timber (CLT). When it was finished, it became the tallest laminated timber structure in Spain.

In terms of reducing demand, the floor area of homes with higher thermal requirements has been limited. Passive bioclimatic strategies have also been implemented to the greatest possible extent, such as the greenhouse on top of the courtyard that allows for the capture of solar radiation in winter, and provides a chimney effect to aid ventilation in summer.

Affordability

One of the cooperative's indispensable principles is to guarantee access to decent and affordable housing. Our response consisted of a two-phase construction plan designed to minimise initial investment. The first phase centres on the completion of the minimum living space needed. In the second, the community add the desired finishing touches over time. Low-tech solutions have been incorporated into the design of the building, in order to accommodate DIY in specific tasks involved in the completion of building work.

From pilot to public policy

La Borda was a pilot project that has now become public policy in Barcelona. In recent years, the City Council has organised two competitions and signed an agreement with nonprofit organisations to offer plots to organised groups and extend the cooperative model.

PRACTICE CASE STUDY

Collaboration for a Home

Retrouvius and Archio

Tennis Court House

Opposite: The barn-like gable cantilevers out from its podium.

Private house newbuilds are full of challenges, especially when clients have never designed a home before. But for Maria Speake, design director of Retrouvius, the dream retirement home she was creating for a family friend and his wife in a neglected corner of a country house garden turned not just complicated but tragic when the wife, the main driver of the project, was diagnosed with cancer and then – having worked tirelessly with Speake to get the project through planning permission – died. But Speake's practice is all about knowing when and where to leave room for manoeuvre. And on this occasion, she told her bereaved client to forget about the project completely and give himself time to recover. Two years later, he came back full of determination to make it happen, but by that time the in-house architect, who had helped draw up all the necessary structural and architectural details to get the project through planning, had left.

So, in a fashion rather similar to her talent for collaging homes together from unlikely but inspired parts, Speake decided, on being introduced to Kyle Buchanan of Archio, to bring him on to the project. Private homes are not Archio's focus, which is primarily social and community-led housing. For Archio it was a shift from the norm that Speake, as interior designer, was in the role of client lead, but possibly more of a challenge was to meet her ambition to insert interesting, found elements into the scheme wherever possible. It should be explained here that Retrouvius, the business Speake and her husband Adam Hills set up in 1993, is driven by the salvaging and either selling on or redeployment in their own schemes of preloved elements of buildings and furniture. Although Speake completed her architectural education (at Glasgow's Mackintosh School of Architecture, where she and Hills met) and they have designed and incorporated successfully into their own elegant home such items as discarded school windows, cheeseboards as ceiling panels and cast-off slabs of marble on floors and walls, she says of this complex newbuild:

I needed someone who thinks and approaches things in a much more architectural way than my sort of reactive way.

I'm very reactive to site, and on the whole I'm very reactive to how clients respond to site. I like to design and then – even though everything is costed up – leave flexibility within certain elements of the design to change as we go along. I mean, 90% of clients can't read a plan. But when they are in the structure they might say: 'I want a window there, so I can see the birds.' Or 'Actually I've always wanted to have a gin and tonic while catching the last bit of western light.' But that's quite difficult on a newbuild.

Archio's response, says co-director Kyle Buchanan, was:

... to make sure we could build flexibility into our detailed design information to allow collaborative discussions to take place between Retrouvius, ourselves, the contractor and of course the client, whilst on site. In many ways that process was the most interesting in terms of collaboration. Our general approach was to be really specific about things we knew the design team wanted

The house is wrapped in timber shingles.

(stone walling, timber shingles, windows, etc.), and also really specific about which areas were going to see more design development during the build, such as balcony handrails, or lighting layouts or certain key materials. All in all I think that process worked well as it allowed the contractor to price things accurately and for the QS to put in appropriate provisional sums where needed.

Speake says:

Kyle referred to me as a design disruptor. I don't know what it means but I like it.

Archio co-director Mellis Haward adds:

What helped was there's a real crossover in values between our two design practices. We work hard as a practice to make sure the homes we design really fit the genuine lived experience of people. For Maria it's about how enjoyable and textural and personal it is. She's so creative with her use of found materials.

So how did that push and pull work in practice? Perhaps it's best to describe the project itself: the site changes level steeply by almost a whole storey across its slope, with a sunken tennis court at the lower end, which is a key feature for the client as he had played tennis there in his childhood.

As per Retrouvius's original design, a lower ground floor, with three bedrooms and bathrooms, sits alongside the tennis court, facing south towards a stream and the historic town. Its walls are constructed with local Cotswold stone, largely repurposed from other buildings on the site. Set on top of this is the main block comprising the kitchen/dining/living area, with a huge window at one end, slightly cantilevered out over the lower ground floor, looking on to the tennis court.

An existing small stone barn to the rear has been refurbished and turned into an annex, intersecting with the main house via a glazed link.

One of Archio's key choices for the main block – which the planners had proposed should be slate – was to wrap cedar shingles around the outside, chosen to fade to a similar shade as the stone below. This is part of the home's interesting mix of materials, which includes Speake's choice of steel trusses. Says Haward:

A more obvious solution would have been timber. But I think the steel was a beautiful way of making the space sing. And it's a modern version of a traditional timber truss. The balustrade details are also more elaborate than we'd have chosen, but we trust Maria that they'll settle in over time. That's a key factor: trust. We trusted her vision and she trusted us, not just to draw it up, but translate it and make it buildable and within budget.

Speake also determined that the main building would have no door frames, to accommodate her client's height – well over 2m tall. So the interior of the main living area is completely open to the pitched roof.

The Tennis Court House sits on a steeply sloping site.

Above right: The interior aesthetic was guided by materials that were already available.

Above left: Joinery is wrapped in suede to create a warmer environment.

Opposite top: The newbuild structure is designed with flexibility in mind.

Opposite bottom: The construction process and interiors are conceived as a cycle, with a material's end-of-life in mind.

There is less of the reclaimed and salvaged material than Speake might ordinarily like, but compromises had to be made for the sake of expediency and budget. The pale pine floorboards are salvaged, and engineered for underfloor heating.

The joinery in the master bedroom and dressing room is wrapped in a soft suede that Speake rescued from a commercial upholsterer. There are reclaimed parquet panels on cabinet doors and kitchen cupboards, and former laboratory counters made of iroko wood used as desktops and for shelves 'to add a touch of warmth and softness', says Speake.

Through the combination of trust and good communication, the necessary flexibility and clarity was achieved. What this unusual team – with the added expertise of their local building contractor – have delivered for their client is a spacious, distinctive and charming home responsive to its immediate site, its wider landscape and, above all, the needs and tastes of the client.

PRACTICE CASE STUDY

Bringing Home to the Unknown

POoR Collective

Opposite: Activated space – climbing frame.

Bringing Home to the Unknown was a vibrant public realm installation located in Regent's Park in London that was co-designed by Year 10 students from Mayesbrook Park School, an alternative school provision in Barking and Dagenham. For the project, Power Out of Restriction Collective worked collaboratively with the RIBA to empower young people.

Founded in 2019, POoR Collective is a social enterprise that focuses on the development of communities through the elevation of young people. The organisation prides itself on its genuine care for communities, youth and those often neglected in society. POoR sees the power of the young generation and seeks to get young voices heard. The founding members are each from working-class backgrounds and recognise the benefits of youth-focused agency in the built environment.

For Bringing Home to the Unknown, POoR Collective worked with a group of Year 10 students from Mayesbrook Park School over six weeks for the RIBA Architecture Ambassador Programme. This is an innovative initiative that pairs architecture professionals with teachers to deliver creative workshops. Across six weeks, POoR taught the students about the built environment through money management, model-making and orthographic drawing exercises to rapidly upskill them so that they could have the confidence to co-design an installation.

By the end of the sessions the students had developed an impressive portfolio of work, which included plans, collages and sketches. Students explored how architecture affects daily life and proposed public realm interventions through sketching and collaging. They then went on to develop their ideas to create the Bringing Home to the Unknown installation in Regent's Park.

Right: Activated space – hide and seek.

Opposite: Activated Space – tag – you're it!

The name stems from the students coming from Greater London and not feeling welcome in central London despite being only a tube ride away from Zone 1. They desired a purpose-built space where they felt welcome, and could dwell and interact with their peers. A home away from home.

The colourful installation encapsulates how the young people from Mayesbrook Park wished to dwell, interact and play. Students embarked on a journey of discovery, which led them to consider what the city meant to them. The design of the installation centred around three key points:

- The idiosyncrasies of outer London versus the homogeneity of central London
- The elements of dwelling: space, seating and shelter
- The methods of taking up space and using your voice to create places

Bringing Home to the Unknown is a series of sculptural benches protected by four circular canopies. Intricately arranged in a circle, the benches form a unique zone for dwelling while the canopies provide much-needed shelter from the elements. They also act as an invitation for young people to dwell and take up the space as they see fit.

Different types of interaction with peers, mentors and family are explored within each of the seats, and each bench invites a distinct and focused experience of what it means to take up space as a young person.

The curated experiences the benches offer comes from the ideas and preferences expressed by the individual students. Some benches encourage a meaningful conversation between two best friends. Others place the occupier in a voyeuristic role where

Right: Activated Space – time to relax.

Opposite: POoR Collective with the students and teachers of Mayesbrook Park School.

Left and below: Co-design workshops with the students of Mayesbrook Park School.

Opposite: POoR Collective members at Bringing Home to the Unknown.

they can watch the world go by. The installation itself stands as a monument to the very idea of young people being allowed a say in how they are treated, and enabled by the built environment once their inherent skills are recognised and their voices are elevated.

Within their practice, POoR use a strategy of genuine engagement to develop creative outcomes. Their process promotes ownership, empowerment and knowledge-sharing.

The social enterprise sees engagement and co-design as an empowerment tool for communities and, as a result, uses interactive workshops as a way to understand how to support local people. This helps to promote ownership in the local area. Local communities have specific needs, and as such POoR is always interested in understanding a site deeply by working with local traders, businesses and talent and promoting citizens in the area. As a result, physical interventions are meaningfully and genuinely co-designed with various stakeholders, community groups, local artists, schools and thinkers. Key elements of the project are always identified for their potential social value and should be co-designed with prominent members and organizations that truly represent the community.

POoR aims to engage, empower and enthuse the custodians of local areas. They acknowledge and tap into the existing creative and entrepreneurial skills of communities and work alongside young people. The London-based collective seeks to give a voice to the disenfranchised by giving them a sense of belonging and creating an ongoing dialogue with the people connecting to local activists and grassroots organisations.

Final Word

Co-producing the future – Is there any other way?

Stephen Hill

Left: A relaxing afternoon in Phoenix Park.

Above: Members of the residents' forum taking a break from their work.

What do you do when a member of your own family asks: 'What is co-production?' Is there a moment of sheer panic? There's no time to rehearse the 3,424 words and 30 slides from my keynote to the RIBA's 2021 Guerrilla Tactics conference.[1] How to capture a lifetime of professional practice ... in about 15 seconds? 'Well, it's complicated ...' is a bit of a cop-out, so maybe this: 'Co-production means existing holders of power and influence, and people who traditionally have had little, recognising that they can, or must, work together to produce something that neither can achieve on their own.' Fourteen seconds, phew! 'Oh, right. I can see why you get so worked up about it.' I do go on rather a lot about citizen empowerment.

It is more complicated than that. How do you create the conditions when co-production is accepted as the necessary process to make something happen, when the powerful may be resistant and those without power sceptical? But even that question highlights the essence of co-production. It describes human relationships (which tend to be messy) and the interactions that flow from whatever is the issue that brings them together, or up against each other. What is that issue, that question? In essence, it will surely always be 'How shall we live ... together ... in an uncertain future?' Isn't that the ultimate question that lies within the brief of any design project? That is a complicated question.

Professional life is just about to get more complicated still, as designers get to grips with the next stage of technology-led design development, with the 'golden thread' of design responsibility for building safety, and the discipline of digital twins. Both are necessary and long overdue, but there is also a real risk that, while the designers and producers of buildings will be collaborating more efficiently and effectively than ever before, they might lose the golden thread of their common humanity with those who live in and use the buildings and places being made.

Making co-production or co-design normal rather than exceptional

'Seeing it is believing it' is an excellent way to learn. But 'feeling it is understanding it' is even better. The 'feeling' shines through in my recent conversation with Amandeep Singh Kalra, architect at Be First, talking about the experience of co-designing Phoenix Park: a meanwhile-use outdoor community space, co-designed with the residents, providing 995 m² of play, exercise, growing and performance space below.

Amandeep, tell me about Phoenix Park

The park sits within the Gascoigne West neighbourhood regeneration, next to Barking town centre. The project is being carried out by Be First, the London Borough of Barking and Dagenham's housebuilding company, and will operate for a three- to five-year period. It was built with supply-chain generosity and a volunteer workforce. It is a testament to the genuine co-design between residents and many other stakeholders, fostering lasting relationships.

How did this co-production process get started?

Well, I started with no experience of what I was embarking on, but it was clear in my mind that we had this fantastic opportunity to create a meanwhile park. I wanted the residents to wholly design it and be the guardians of it. 'They will make it too ambitious ... we won't be able to deliver it ... and we don't want to disappoint them.' These are some of the common things clients say when the idea emerges of decentralising design responsibility to people that would actually use those spaces. It's all absolute rubbish.

So what happened then?

We gave the residents all the tools: design support, budget, sustainability, stewardship. We filled the room with experts: landscape architects, contractors, client, and maintenance teams. But what then came from residents was exponentially better in creating a park that best suited their needs. On paper this seems straightforward, and I expected the result to be great. What I had not grasped was the impact the process would have on me personally, and all those professionals involved. Satisfaction in supporting residents to shape their local neighbourhood replaced the ego revolving around 'owning ideas'. The sense of satisfaction being 'the designer' was out the window.

What would you say to other organisations thinking about co-production, but nervous of the unknown, and the risks?

This project was intense and resource-heavy but, contrary to popular myth, it didn't cost a lot. Why? When people do things they enjoy, they are generous with their time. This project was built with hundreds of hours of volunteer time because it was enjoyable.

Enjoyable? Is that enough of a justification?

Well, as clients we have now embedded co-design into all future projects. The landscape architects approach every new client, and ask them to co-design it, even when they haven't been asked to. The contractors want more projects like this with us.

And how did your other co-producers feel about it?
At the end of the project, we asked the residents involved how they felt. One, in particular, really touched me: 'Barking is changing more than ever before, and the borough really cares about putting the local community at the centre of the change. Before the Gascoigne residents' forum, I had the polar opposite opinion of the council ... my entire life.'

That's a definite win, then?
Yes, the park is undeniably fantastic, but for me the real story here is the way the process has impacted the lives of all those involved. I believe its power is only truly understood by those who have experienced it. I just wish someone had told me about co-design before!

Co-production means working in a different way and doing different things

As Amandeep Singh Kalra experienced and observed, co-production touches people in many ways: as a route to community agency and professional and personal self-actualisation; as effective sharing of knowledge, experience and ideas; and as purposeful creativity and innovation for an uncertain but hopefully better future: above all, it is a life-enhancing experience.

Co-production also needs to be understood by designers as abandoning the search for the 'perfect moment', when all the brief requirements, design assumptions and compromises might improbably work 'as designed'. Instead, design becomes the starting point for possibilities, and for adaptations to how we might want to (or have to) live in the future. RIBA guidance for architects working on Neighbourhood Plans[2] made this same point over a decade ago: 'The challenge for designers is not to design a finite scheme based on assumptions about future behaviour ... but to provide a foundation from which residents carry on designing through living in the place, as an intentional community.'

Co-production is therefore a way into a quite different method of working. The role of designer as facilitator is critical in the early stages, particularly as 'project' rather than 'building' designer; helping design how the project itself will work. The physical and psychological occupation of space and attachment to place is then the ongoing activity of 'design by living': the stage in which most professional designers rarely play any long-term role. This has been a significant gap in professional learning. Post-occupation research can remedy some of this, but perhaps digital twinning will also be able to capture long-term experiential data about how places work and how people feel about living and working in them.

The urban sociologist Richard Sennett has had a lifelong preoccupation with 'the open city',[3] recognising the necessity for building citizen and professional agency into the design and management of the cities of the future. He describes the city both as a 'built environment' and as 'how people dwell in it'. He sees 'the closed city' as a reaction to the 20th-century 'horror of disorder', over-determined but 'brittle', unable to achieve the planned equilibrium and integration promised by 'an arsenal of technological tools ... which urbanists even a hundred years ago could not begin to imagine'. Contrast that with the open city of our lived experience of 'ambiguous edges ... incomplete form ... unresolved narrative', and in which planning and design 'attends to conflicts and possibilities ... problem solving ... problem finding, [and] discovery rather than merely clarity'.

Sennett is not a practical planner or co-producer, but his vision for the role of the whole city designer is as it needs to be for each of the city's working parts: to shape the process of discovery for meanwhile parks, a street or a whole residential neighbourhood,[4] whatever. The activist urban designer Robert Goodman, supporting communities affected by 'the urban crisis' in North American cities in the 1970s, challenged planners, architects and engineers to be 'citizen professionals': 'We are, in effect, the client for all our projects, for it is our own society we are affecting through our actions ... By raising the possibilities of a humane way of producing places to live, by phasing out the elitist nature of environmental professionalism, we can move toward a time when we will no longer define ourselves by our profession, but by our freedom as people.'[5] Responding to this challenge is as necessary today as it was half a century ago.

1 Stephen Hill, '*Keynote – collaboration for citizens in the age of the digital twin*', RIBA Guerrilla Tactics conference: Stop, Collaborate, Listen, November 2021, PowerPoint presentation: https://riba.app.box.com/s/fqvnleo1gtwox314enly63g2w7vaypgo/file/882863584152 (both accessed 1 March 2022).
2 Marilyn Taylor and Stephen Hill, 'Community housing: Co-producing good places', *RIBA Guide to Localism: Opportunities for Architects: Part 1 Neighbourhood Planning*, RIBA, 2011, http://www.fluidoffice.com/wp-content/uploads/2014/01/0420-RIBA-Guide-Part-1.pdf (accessed 1 March 2022).
3 Richard Sennett, 'The open city', November 2006, https://urbanage.lsecities.net/essays/the-open-city (accessed 1 March 2022); Richard Sennett, *Building and Dwelling: Ethics for the City*, Allen Lane, 2018.
4 Metropolitan Workshop, 'People powered places', 2020–1, https://metwork.co.uk/research/people-powered-places/ (accessed 1 March 2022); issuu, 'Prospects paper #2 – people powered places', April 2021, https://issuu.com/metropolitanworkshop/docs/mw_prospects_publication_02_210422/40 (accessed 1 March 2022) – including the author's paper on co-producing cooperative and cohousing housing developments, pp31–3.
5 Robert Goodman, *After the Planners*, Penguin, 1972. Stephen Hill read selected extracts during the Architecture Foundation's 100 Day Studio Bedtime Stories, August 2020, https://www.youtube.com/watch?v=If7dIWWmjaM&list=PL4mkZZN7AjRF1b9jtbPv_m2kXCbXRoIKv&index=28&ab_channel=ArchitectureFoundation (accessed 1 March 2022).

Contributors

Dhruv Adam Sookhoo is a chartered architect, chartered town planner, and Visiting Lecturer at the School of Architecture, Planning and Landscape, Newcastle University, where he completed a PhD examining the social practices adopted by architects to realise housing quality during development management. He is former Head of Research and Practice Innovation, Metropolitan Workshop; Head of Design, Home Group; and Chair of the RIBA Housing Group.

Sarah Ahmed is an architectural assistant at Archio. She has worked on a number of housing and masterplanning projects for Plus Architecture in Dublin and co-founded the Sudan Art and Design Library Project, where she is currently head of research.

Dr Joe Jack Williams is an Associate and researcher at FCBStudios and co-leads environmental research for the practice, identifying, developing and enabling research across sectors and projects. He is a Certified Passivhaus Consultant.

WIP Collaborative is a shared feminist practice of independent design professionals working together on projects that engage community and the public realm.

Siri Zanelli is an architect with built work published internationally. Her many years in Japan nurtured her passion for compact housing and unexpected design solutions. She has led timber housing projects from idea through to completion, and always finds a way to add a bit more colour, texture and joy; the human touch, to any project.

Khuzema Hussain is excellent at finding the technical solution to a complex problem. He has been focused on the construction of single family and multi-unit housing for the past decade. Prior to that he helped deliver complex office buildings and exhibition halls. Khuzema currently supports projects over RIBA Stages 4, 5 & 6 and is an associate for the Design Council's Network of Experts.

Alasdair Ben Dixon is a chartered architect and steering group member within Architects Declare. He has long-held a commitment to the needs of the wider community alongside clients and stakeholders. This passion has led to roles within charities and action groups alongside his work in practice. He contributed to the RIBA Ethics and Sustainable Development commission, and regularly speaks publicly on such topics.

Tomas Tvarijonas is an architect with international project experience in residential, commercial, and cultural sectors. His field of interest is robotic manufacturing in the construction industry, which he has been pursuing as academic research and commercial application. Before joining Collective Works, he worked at RSHP and lectured at The Bartlett School of Architecture.

Marc Cairns is Managing Director of New Practice. He is a founding Director along with Becca Thomas. Marc leads on new collaborations, new clients, new projects and new challenges. He also leads on the public facing aspect of the practice, reinforcing our particular design approach by regularly presenting to peers and wider audiences, and lectures internationally. Marc is also an

Associate at the Design Council and leads ArchitectureLGBT+ in Scotland.

Samuel Stair is a Senior Designer at New Practice. Since joining New Practice in 2021 he has worked on projects from concept to delivery including a major public facing exhibition and events space for COP26 and a heritage anchored masterplan for Glasgow's oldest High Street. Samuel regularly contributes to academic writing and thinking, and is co-founder of Chez Etym.

David Ogunmuyiwa is founder of architecture and urban design practice ArchitectureDoingPlace, specialising in arts and regeneration projects.
He is a Mayor's Design Advocate and Historic England Expert Advisory Group member. He teaches and mentors widely and has practiced architecture in the UK and the Middle East. He is a confirmed urbanist.

Matthew Morris is an Architectural Technologist at Hawkins\Brown Architects and has worked across a broad range of projects, from concept through to construction and delivery. He is part of the UK Green Building Council's expert led task group on whole life carbon reductions and is developing national construction sector standards for the circular economy with the British Standards Institute. At Architects Climate Action Network Matthew coordinates the Circular Economy Group, successfully delivering the Circular Series and now leading the Circular Economy design guide publication.

Lanre Gbolade is an architect and Co-Founder of Gbolade Design Studio, an award-winning architecture and sustainable design practice based in London. In 2017, he co-founded Paradigm Network with four industry friends and colleagues to champion Black & Asian representation and visibility of ethnically diverse-led businesses within the built environment.

Amy Francis-Smith is a multi-award-winning Disabled Architect, Inclusive Designer and Consultant for Accessible Architecture, Project Lead at Pinnegar Hayward Design and the outgoing Vice-President of the Birmingham Architectural Association. Campaigning for legislative change, her work and research focuses on providing decent accommodations for people with Disabilities. An RIBAJ Rising Star, an Archiboo Activism winner, shortlisted for the National Diversity Award's - Positive Disability Role Model, and named on the Shaw Trust's Power 100 as one of the UK's most influential Disabled people.

Lacol is a cooperative of architects based in Barcelona that works to generate community infrastructures for the sustainability of life, as a key tool for the eco-social transition, through architecture, cooperativism and participation. It has been awarded with several recognitions, including the Emerging category of the EU Mies van der Rohe Awards 2022, and has been selected in the biennials of architecture in Venice (2016, 2021), Buenos Aires (2017) and San Sebastián (2019).

Retrouvius is driven by the belief that good materials and well-made things are precious. The Retrouvius story began in the mid-nineties as a reaction to the horror of demolition witnessed in Glasgow when the founders Adam and Maria were studying. Now, housed across in Kensal Green,

Retrouvius increasingly understands its mission to be something more fundamental: to enable and inspire reuse, not just as a design preference, but as an attitude, principled process and a way of life.

Archio imagines a better quality of life for everyone. They think that access to decent homes, buildings and spaces provides the foundation to help us grow as individuals and as communities. The practice was founded with a mindset that design should be used to tackle major societal challenges. They seek out opportunities to progressively shape a better, more sustainable and more inclusive world for now, and for future generations.

POoR is a social enterprise that focuses on the development of communities through the elevation of young people. POoR sees the power of the younger generation and seeks to get young voices heard. Through knowledge sharing and design, POoR aims to bridge the gap between communities, bring together a wealth of demographics, and empower the youth of today.

Stephen Hill is a public interest practitioner working in the commercial, governmental and non-profit housing sectors, focused on equitable and sustainable development, community engagement, strategic urban planning, project design and action learning. Strong research and innovation record on participative democracy and more sustainable forms of housing delivery and ownership, including a Churchill Fellowship to USA and Canada to examine different approaches to community organising and the co-production by the state and citizens of housing and neighbourhood-scale developments. Instrumental in the growth of the UK community land trust and cohousing national bodies. Originally qualified as a planning and development surveyor andland economist, he also teaches professional ethics to mid-career built environment design and development professionals.

Opposite: La Borda, Barcelona, 2018. La Borda's south facade seen from the future park of Can Batlló.

tic tac Ca Batlló
VOLEM CAN BATLLÓ, JA!!!

Recommended Reading and Resources

Books

Blundell Jones, P., Petrescu, D., Till, J., *Architecture and Participation*, Routledge, 2005.

Dove, C., *Radical Housing: Designing Multigenerational + Co-Living Housing for All*, RIBA Publishing, 2020.

Publica, *Vital Neighbourhoods: Lessons from international housing renewal*, 2017.

Ed. Pamela Buxton, *New Architects 4*, The Architecture Foundation, 2021.

Harriss, H., Hyde, R., Marcaccio, R., *Architects After Architecture: Alternative Pathways for Practice*, Routledge, 2020.

Institutes and Initiatives

Architects Climate Action Network
www.architectscan.org

FCBS CARBON
https://fcbstudios.com/fcbscarbon

London Architects Group
https://londonarchitectsgroup.org

London Practice Forum
https://practiceforum.london

Paradigm Network
www.paradigmnetwork.co.uk

POoR Collective
www.poorcollective.com

Parlour
https://parlour.org.au

Articles

Bertoli, R., Stathaki, E., 'Architecture and design activism strives for a better future Architecture and design activism strives for a better future', *Wallpaper**, <https://www.wallpaper.com/architecture/architecture-design-activism-initiatives>, 2021.

Haward, M., 'Want to make architecture useful again? Collaborate, collaborate, collaborate', *Architects' Journal*, <https://www.architectsjournal.co.uk/news/opinion/want-to-make-architecture-useful-again-collaborate-collaborate-collaborate 4>, 2021.

RIBAJ, 'Guerrilla Tactics: Collaboration is good for everyone', *RIBAJ*, <https://www.ribaj.com/intelligence/riba-nbs-guerrilla-tactics-collaboration>, 2021.

McEwen, H., Stewart, C., 'In It Together: how collaboration benefits practices large and small', *RIBAJ*, <https://www.ribaj.com/intelligence/rising-stars-column-hugh-mcewen-catrina-stewart-office-s-m-collaboration>, 2020.

Beaumont, E., 'Lacol Arquitectura Cooperativa: "We collaborate with different causes, as neighbours"', *Architectural Review*, <https://www.architectural-review.com/archive/lacol-arquitectura-cooperativa-we-collaborate-with-different-causes-as-neighbours>, 2019.

Brandon, E., 'Restorative Ground is an all-ages playground for neurodiversity', *Fast Company*, <https://www.fastcompany.com/90662691/how-cities-can-be-redesigned-for-neurodiversity>, 2021.

Index

Page numbers in **bold** indicate figures.

Image Credits

vii, viii
RIBA
1, 3
Chris Snook Photography
2, 8
Metropolitan Workshop
5, 6, 7
Taran Wilkhu Photography
12-20
Archio
23-26
Feilden Clegg Bradley Studios
30-32, 34-38
WIP Collaborative
33
WIP Collaborative / Hudson Square
40 top, 42 bottom
Thomas Broadhead
40 bottom, 44
Keaton Chau
41, 45 top
Nina Mucalov
42 top, 46
Collective Works
42 bottom, 43
Amandine Allesandra
45 bottom
Will Hearle
48
New Practice
50
Sadie St. Hilaire / New Practice
52, 55
Spike Wright / New Practice
53
RESOLVE Collective / New Practice
54
Will Scott / New Practice
58-62
David Ogunmuyiwa
64-66
Marta Catillo
68
ACAN / Keith van Loen
69
Kate Raworth
70, 72
ACAN
71
ACAN / Pablo Llopis
74-78
Paradigm Network
80
Paul Painter
83, 86 top
Amy Francis-Smith
84
Grazia UK
86 bottom
Thom Bartley
87
Archiboo
89-92
Lacol
93
Álvaro Valdecantos
94-95
Lluc Miralles
97-103
Theo Tennant
105, 107, 108, 109, 111
Luke O'Donovan
110
POoR Collective
112
Amandeep Singh Kalra
121
Chopo